Outside In

Outside In

Thoughtful interiors inspired by the natural world

Lauren Camilleri and Sophia Kaplan

For our young gardeners – Rafi, Otis, Frankie and Jack

We take great pride in acknowledging the Gadigal people of the Eora Nation as the Traditional Custodians of the land on which we have written this book. For more than 60,000 years First Nations people have been intrinsically linked to the land, to nature and to the bounty of flora and fauna that surrounds us. There are many lessons to be learned from their knowledge and experience. We pay our deepest respects to Elders both past and present. Always was, always will be.

Contents

Foreword

Georgina Reid, founding editor of *Wonderground* (formerly *The Planthunter*)

As many landscape architects and designers can attest, the garden has traditionally been at the bottom of the home making and reshaping pecking order. Sometimes as an afterthought, other times as a non-essential budget item, or even an indulgence. Not anymore, and certainly not in the striking projects featured in this book.

This book documents a movement, return and realisation that is green and wild and abundant. It is this, beautifully articulated by cultural anthropologist Natasha Myers in *Wonderground*: 'Plants are integral to what it means to be human. We are only because they are.' Through this lens and throughout this book, a garden is not an afterthought, and nature is not a place to visit somewhere 'out there'. It's right here – on our windowsills and in our living rooms, courtyards, balconies and backyards.

Though it is so obvious as to almost sound trite, it's worth repeating that we exist in deep, often unseen, connection with *all* life. While many of us spend our days staring at screens in air-conditioned buildings many metres off the ground, the truth of our embeddedness remains. Increasingly, it's illustrated through scientific research. Sue Stuart-Smith points to this in *The Well Gardened Mind* where she writes of experiments documenting the 'pro social' effects of nature. 'People behave better and connect with one another more when they are in the presence of plants and trees.' This is true even when we are only in the presence of indoor plants or images showing scenes of nature. When research participants were asked to make decisions in this context, as opposed to an environment with no greenery, they showed higher levels of generosity and trust. Not only do plants make us human, sharing our lives with them makes us *better* humans.

We live in incredibly unsteady times. Crises abound – climate, biodiversity, ecological, extinction, geopolitical – you name it, here we are. It's easy to feel impotent and to dismiss small actions in favour of grand techno-fixes, but the complexity of the situation we're in requires all scales of thinking and acting: global, regional, local. As David Orr writes in the essay 'What is Education For?' the world is calling for 'people who live well in their places' – people who are committed to caring deeply for the place they live in and the beings they share it with. A wise gardener once told me that although making a garden is not going to address climate change or offset global extinction rates, it will make a huge difference to the lives of the species inhabiting the site. 'You've done something,' he said. 'It's not small, it might just seem small to you.'

This book is a glorious invitation to rethink the way we design, and live, with plants; to transform the design process into a circle, not a straight line. To begin with place and life and abundance, and end with place and life and abundance. Because gardening is not just about making things beautiful, it's a radical act of care and connection in a world in desperate need of both.

Introduction

As humans, we are intrinsically drawn to the natural world: nourished, revitalised and inspired by its beauty and vitality. It makes sense that the spaces we inhabit should explore and foster this relationship. From inner-city residences that use internal courtyards to bring light and life to a home to larger buildings that fit seamlessly into their landscape, *Outside In* investigates how architects, interior designers and landscape designers explore and resolve our desire to be close to nature.

At their best, the spaces we live and work in can shape and enhance our lives in the most wonderful way. More than just serving a purely functional purpose of providing shelter from the elements or somewhere to rest our head, great architecture and design can make us happier and healthier. The inclusion of green spaces plays a huge role. Design that is in harmony with nature is good for us and our environment alike. A connection to the natural world doesn't just help us appreciate its beauty, it encourages us to take better care of it by being mindful of the choices we make in our everyday lives.

Outside In features twenty-five projects that go well beyond the mere inclusion of houseplants or a traditional backyard. In creating the spaces in this book, the architects, interior designers and landscape designers have placed garden and landscape at the forefront of the process, using them to guide their designs. These projects draw inspiration from nature that exceeds the aesthetic, adding value to the lives of both their occupants and the surrounding environment.

A connection to the natural world doesn't just help us appreciate its beauty, it encourages us to take better care of it by being mindful of the choices we make in our everyday lives.

Although this isn't a book specifically about biophilia (a theory introduced by Professor Edward O. Wilson in his 1986 book *Biophilia*, which posits that humans have a biological need to be connected to nature), many of its principles are relevant here. Most of our lives are now spent in the built environment rather than the natural one, and biophilic design explores the way architecture can integrate natural elements that contribute to our health and wellbeing.

Biophilic design emphasises natural ventilation and light, easy access to indoor and outdoor gardens, natural colours and materials, organic shapes, calming water features and views to greenery. When combined, these elements create 'healthier' spaces that promote positive and enduring interactions with nature.

Merrick's Farmhouse (p. 66) incorporates many of these design elements. This rural home is built around a courtyard that can be viewed from every space in the house. It allows light and air to flow through the building, and its pools and ponds add tranquillity and calm. This central outdoor room is a meeting place for family and friends and greatly enhances the overall design of the home.

The psychological and physical benefits of green spaces are no small thing. Views of plants, and interactions with them, have been shown to have a calming effect that can reduce stress and boost productivity. The benefits of tending to a garden are innumerable – from the physical exertion and meditative nature of its maintenance to the satisfaction of seeing it thrive. Being in nature calms the mind, sparks delight and helps us appreciate the natural cycle of life and death.

In creating the restorative wellness space Sense of Self (p. 112), the design team took inspiration from nature and the healing properties of water and made generous use of plants to encourage interactions between the guests and their surroundings. The balance between the structure of the built environment and the organic nature of plants creates a beautiful aesthetic tension. The living element softens any robust materials and strong angles, adding power to both. Plants keep us deeply connected to the seasons, allowing us to witness the passing of time in the most poetic of ways. From bare stems and bulbs pushing forth in winter to the joy of early spring days, with fresh green leaves unfurling and hints of warmer weather to come. In summer we experience a sometimes erratic and overwhelming abundance, when flowers compete for attention from pollinators and grasses grow tall. As the season shifts to autumn, deciduous trees, such as the Japanese maple found growing inside the home at River House (p. 162), put on a show of brightly coloured leaves and remind us to prepare for cooler weather ahead.

Many of the homes featured in this book do not aim to be perfectly sealed vessels, but are open to the environment, connecting the residents to the weather and allowing it to play a role in daily life. At Sunday (p. 134), occupants regularly pass through a central open courtyard that separates the public and private realms of the house. Rain or shine, they are aware of the external conditions. Daily activities are more considered, as the home elevates and ritualises the living experience.

At Garden House (p. 124), every effort has been made to tread lightly on the site. A process to regenerate the indigenous vegetation began and the location of the building was subsequently chosen to cover a patch of land that failed to thrive. The structure sits on a raised platform that allows wildlife to travel across the site unimpeded. Similarly, at Edgeland House (p. 184), a rooftop garden was developed to restore the original sloping of the landscape and heal the scars of the site's industrial past.

It's heartening to see a growing trend towards the use of indigenous species. Many of the gardens featured in this book are a testament to that, and there are a multitude of positive outcomes from their inclusion. Selecting plants that occur naturally within the ecosystem of a site ensures their vigour and offers a true regeneration of the land without the need for pesticides or synthetic fertilisers. It also provides the best environment for local fauna.

At Fisherman's House (p. 228), the architects and landscape designers were intent on creating a respectful restoration of the waterfront cottage and surrounding land. An ecological study of the site was undertaken, and the remnant vegetation was restored, eventually leading to a beautiful garden that has helped to regenerate the foreshore forest and coastal heath habitats originally found in the area.

Gardens also play an important role in maintaining biodiversity within built environments. Healthy soil indicates an active underground world of worms, insects, mycelium and bacteria. A mere teaspoon of healthy soil contains more than a billion important microbes. Together they work hard, day in, day out, to break down organic matter and return nutrients to the soil. These actions, and those of plant roots, allow the soil to sequester carbon and effectively absorb rain, meaning cleaner air and a decreased likelihood of erosion and flooding. Above ground, plants are also busy absorbing carbon dioxide, releasing oxygen in return. Their leaves and branches provide food and shelter for a vast array of wildlife, from local birds to insects and even small marsupials. Now more than ever, sustainability should be at the forefront of our minds. Buildings that prioritise green space, employ passive design principles to help limit their environmental impact, use sustainable materials and show a reverence for nature in general are essential for addressing the climate crisis.

The owner and designer of Ground House 107R (p. 86) was adamant that the building should recede into the landscape so as not to impose on its environment. After enlarging a natural amphitheatre on the site, building into this space and incorporating a rooftop garden, the house almost disappears into its green surroundings. It is beautifully grounded in its site. Similarly, House of the Big Arch (p. 220), with its mission to save all existing trees on the site, sits ensconced in its mountainous bush location, providing shelter for its occupants and local wildlife alike.

Collaboration is at the heart of many of these projects, both in the design process and the ongoing function of the spaces. Daylesford Longhouse (p. 16) is a thoughtful example of architecture bringing people together. The building hosts creative workshops and a cooking school and is a haven for those who want to learn more about the organic sustainable farming practices undertaken there.

Gardens and parks also provide a perfect setting for gathering and interacting. Within our homes and public buildings, green spaces can encourage moments of connection. We are social creatures and we depend on these daily interactions. London's Barbican Conservatory (p. 250) is a wonderful example of urban design that improves the lives of its inhabitants by fostering community. Through combining residential housing with views to greenery, spaces dedicated to cultural experiences, lush communal thoroughfares and a dedicated conservatory, the architects have created a modern neighbourhood experience in central London.

Positively addressing the streetscape of our suburbs and cities can impact the whole community, so it's important that buildings are designed with adequate consideration of how they will be experienced both inside and out. Autumn House (p. 46) has perforated metal screening that will eventually become covered in greenery, offering beauty and privacy for the residents, verdancy to passers-by and flora for local pollinators. In a densely populated commercial district in Tokyo, the plant-filled balconies and terraces of Garden & House (p. 202) create a green oasis in a concrete jungle. It is a moment of reprieve in a decidedly urban locale.

Outside In features a selection of unique projects that have been thoughtfully and meticulously designed and constructed by experts, but this is not the reality for most people. Building or renovating a house with the help of architects and designers is a privilege that only some people have access to. Nevertheless, all these projects offer ideas and lessons that can be applied in different ways at all levels of society.

Everyone should have meaningful access to green space, even in the most urban of locations. This could mean joining a local community garden or lobbying governments to prioritise the inclusion of public green spaces and the preservation of

Architecture that embraces the natural world from the beginning of the design process, and holds it at its core, engenders a more sustainable approach to building and living.

natural habitats over development in our cities. In our local area, residents are encouraged to 'adopt' the verge at the front of their homes by replacing the ubiquitous turf with a garden, creating wildlife habitat and hopefully building community among neighbours. Many cities across the globe have mandated that every newly built flat roof (that isn't designated as a terrace) must include a rooftop garden. These gardens not only help to battle rising temperatures, but also provide better stormwater management, leading to less flooding, and increase precious biodiversity in the city.

A life lived closer to nature is beneficial for individuals and the world at large. Architecture that embraces the natural world from the beginning of the design process, and holds it at its core, engenders a more sustainable approach to building and living. This connection to landscape encourages community and elevates our daily lives. We hope you enjoy discovering these projects and are inspired to use some of the ideas in your own home and life.

Daylesford Longhouse

ELEVATED PLAINS, VICTORIA, AUSTRALIA
COMPLETED 2013

Traditional Owners: Dja Dja Wurrung people of the Kulin Nation

PHOTOGRAPHY
Rory Gardiner and Phillip Huynh

ARCHITECT
Timothy Hill (Partners Hill)

LANDSCAPE DESIGNER
Trace Streeter with Partners Hill masterplan

BUILDER
Nick Andrew Construction

Devised by architect Timothy Hill of Partners Hill, who was commissioned by and worked collaboratively with owners Ronnen Goren and Trace Streeter, along with a slew of other architects, Daylesford Longhouse was a unique proposition from the beginning. Ronnen explains, 'The idea was the culmination of a number of things that brought us to the concept of fashioning a longhouse with everything under one 110-metre-long (361-foot-long) roof. Drawing inspiration from one of our food heroes, Skye Gyngell, and her venture at Petersham Nursery, the thought of having a kitchen, garden and life within the greenhouse (of sorts) brought a heightened connectivity and relationship between people, food and source.'

Right A deliberately small vestibule leads from the expanse of the entry hall/garage to the living, sleeping, cooking and garden spaces. **Below** Swathes of grass grow on mounds that shield the residence from its exposed site. **Opposite** Tuscan kale, nasturtium and an almond tree thrive in the protected surrounds of the translucent, shed-like exterior. **Previous spread** Vines encase a walkway in the timber-heavy interior.

As a home, a working farm and a cooking school, [this] is a hive of creativity and collaboration.

Above A stairway leads to one of the mezzanine areas, which help fill the volume of the shed and house with a lounging area and guest quarters. **Opposite** The productive, working garden provides an abundance of food for the owners and their visitors. **Previous spread** Tree ferns and native ground covers are just part of the diverse plant selection inside the structure.

Right (top) White glazed bricks and contrasting mortar create a robust bathroom. **Right (bottom)** Low-set windows offer a view from the bed. **Opposite** The rugged, exposed site informed the decision to create a giant, shed-like greenhouse to protect the inhabitants, their animals and plants, and the local wildlife from the weather. **Following spread** The large, welcoming kitchen at the heart of Daylesford Longhouse includes a generous dining table and is used to host regular workshops run by the owners and their collaborators.

Sitting on top of an exposed hill close to Daylesford in central Victoria, the building, which sometimes needs to shield its inhabitants from extreme weather conditions, looks from the outside like a massive, long shed. Inside, it is a rich and layered home, replete with an abundant garden and animal pens, all under one roof. The design isn't a purely romantic notion – each element plays a vital role in the functioning of the ecosystem the team have created. Rainwater collected from the expansive roof waters the garden. The animals, who are penned and fed at one end of the building, provide nutrient-rich compost that is aged before being added to the garden, alleviating the need for synthetic fertilisers or supplementary soil.

The garden is a verdant paradise, filled with lush greenery, natives and edibles, that changes with the seasons. The eye is drawn to the thick white blossom of the almond tree (*Prunus amygdalus*) in spring, the deep reds of the Virginia creeper (*Parthenocissus quinquefolia*) in autumn, and the bright orange spikes of the native banksia (*Banksia* sp.) in winter. Native violet (*Viola banksii*), tree ferns, bamboo (*Bambusa* sp.), star jasmine (*Trachelospermum jasminoides*) and the large, kidney-shaped discs of the leopard plant (*Farfugium japonicum*) provide a layer of greenery all year round. For food, there are figs (*Ficus carica*), Tuscan kale (*Brassica oleracea* var. *palmifolia*), passionfruit (*Passiflora edulis*) and caper berries (*Capparis spinosa*) among a vast array of seasonal produce.

This connection to nature is very important to Ronnen and Trace. It exists on many different levels, from nourishing themselves and their guests with the produce they grow through to what Ronnen describes as 'the visual connection to beauty and seasonality that is always present, and being able to see the changes in foliage, flowers and pasture'. He also explains, 'while the ability to put one's hands in soil creates a connection to the environment, it also works at a microbial level'.

As a home, a working farm and a cooking school, Daylesford Longhouse is a hive of creativity and collaboration. More than ten years into its existence, it continues to welcome guests to share in its bounty. Ronnen and Trace's mission is to continue learning and nourishing themselves and their visitors socially, mentally and physically – creating a more sustainable and connected model of living.

AVERY

Chelsea Brut

LONDON, ENGLAND, UK
COMPLETED 2022

PHOTOGRAPHY
Johan Dehlin

Below The new extension has a direct connection with the lush garden through floor-to-ceiling windows. **Opposite** The dense, lush planting of the backyard is complemented by the grassy rooftop garden above. **Previous spread** Sheer curtains allow dappled light into the ground-floor living area, where a LaWo1 lounge chair, designed by Han Pieck for Lawo Ommen, takes pride of place.

Above On the first floor, the full-length windows offer views to the grasses on the rooftop garden of the new extension.
Opposite The canopies of the mature neighbouring trees provide added greenery and privacy.

One of London's more upmarket boroughs, known for its Victorian architecture, Chelsea seems an unlikely location for a row of mid-century townhouses. Sitting within that row of 1960s homes, Chelsea Brut is a unique modernist gem, expertly transformed by UK architects Pricegore. This is a home that embraces the brutalist aesthetic of its origins. A deep dive into the history of the site revealed exciting insights that, coupled with the architects' respect for the heritage of the home, have resulted in the reimagining of the space into a contemporary family residence with a decidedly green edge.

ARCHITECT
Pricegore

LANDSCAPE DESIGNER
FFLO

BUILDER
Allstruct

Above and opposite The neutral internal palette draws the eye to the mature black locust and horse chestnut trees growing outside the stairwell and the master bedroom. **Following spread** Pops of green from the garden, joinery and indoor plants soften the brutalist design.

Known for their sensitive remodelling of heritage homes, Pricegore have demonstrated the same thoughtfulness in their approach to the more recent history of Chelsea Brut. Seeing the project as a collaboration with the building's original architects, Pricegore wanted to honour its origins while adapting and modernising it. Identifying the existing elements worth preserving left them free to rework those that no longer served.

Stripping the house back to its basic elements allowed for necessary improvements to the functionality of the home. Services were upgraded and insulation added throughout along with double glazing to increase the building's thermal properties and energy efficiency. To bring additional natural light into the space and facilitate passive cooling, a large, automated skylight was installed in the roof.

The discovery of remnants of a Victorian terrace beneath the structure provided the most inspired inclusion in the new renovation. Noticing that the gardens of neighbouring properties sat lower than that of the row of townhouses, the architects found that the original foundations of the site were also lower than the more modern ones. This made possible the addition of a lower-ground-floor extension that steps down from the front of the house. By excavating 1.4 metres (4.6 feet) they were able to add significant volume. The resulting high ceilings, coupled with a wall of full-length sliding glass doors at the rear of the new living room, creates a feeling of spaciousness, brings natural light deep into the building and provides a visual connection to the lush garden area beyond.

The space was reconfigured from a five-bedroom house into a more generously proportioned three-bedroom residence that better suited its new owners and their teenage children. Referencing the design of Brazilian brutalist homes, a close relationship between inside and out was vital and reflects the architects' commitment to incorporating nature into urban living. All rooms offer views to greenery, either to the surrounding trees or the landscaping.

Flowing over three levels, the garden – which includes a water feature to help conceal nearby traffic noise – reinforces a sense of serenity that belies the inner-city location. Downstairs, the kitchen and living area looks out to the tropical subterranean garden through floor-to-ceiling glazing. Concrete terracing is planted with tree ferns, various hortensia (*Hydrangea* spp.) and other dappled shade dwellers. Inside, a concrete ledge holds potted indoor plants, including a peacock plant (*Goeppertia orbifolia*) and a mini monstera (*Rhaphidophora tetrasperma*), that enjoy the light that filters in through the more mature trees outside and a round skylight.

The roof over the new extension is planted with grasses that soften the outlook from the first-floor rooms and provide privacy. On the upper floors, housing the bedrooms and master suite, large windows frame views to canopies of honey locust (*Gleditsia triacanthos*), black locust (*Robinia pseudoacacia*) and horse chestnut (*Aesculus hippocastanum*) trees.

The architects have breathed new life into this brutalist townhouse, maximising space, natural light and a connection to nature, while honouring its history. Chelsea Brut is a city home that is cocooned from the busyness of urban life.

All rooms offer views to greenery, either to the surrounding trees or the landscaping.

Green Box

CERIDO, LOMBARDY, ITALY
COMPLETED 2011

PHOTOGRAPHY
Marcello Mariana

Above and opposite The simple galvanised-steel kitchen doubles as a gardening work bench. **Previous spread** European honeysuckle and golden clematis fully envelop the structure.

ARCHITECT
act_romegialli

DESIGN TEAM
Gianmatteo Romegialli and Erika Gaggia

LANDSCAPE DESIGNER
Gheo Clavarino

Green Box, a project designed by Gianmatteo Romegialli and Erika Gaggia, co-founders of the architectural firm act_romegialli, is built onto the bones of a small disused garage that was part of a weekend house on the slopes of the Rhaetian Alps in northern Italy. The ethereal structure appears to be at one with the mountains in which it sits, engulfed in climbing vines. Sometimes wild and sometimes more manicured, Green Box, the architects attest, becomes a 'privileged observation point of the changing of the seasons' within its striking landscape. Retaining its original stone columns, a new concrete roof was added, and lightweight metal and steel wires were wrapped around the volume of the structure, creating a support for a seemingly overgrown yet carefully designed tangle of vines to grow around.

Above and opposite Timber, concrete and the original stone columns are warm and hardwearing, while expansive windows and glazed doors ensure the surrounding greenery is ever-present. **Previous spread** The former garage almost disappears into the alpine landscape.

Landscape designer Gheo Clavarino, who creates gardens full of light, colour and movement, chose deciduous silver lace vine (*Polygonum baldshuanicum*) and European honeysuckle (*Lonicera periclymenum*) to provide a thick covering of green in the warmer months. Golden clematis (*Clematis tangutica*), with its striking bright yellow bell-shaped flowers and fluffy Dr Seuss-esque seed heads, and common hop (*Humulus lupulus*), with its light green cone-shaped flowers, add texture and interest to the jungle of rooftop vines.

Along the base of the structure, a mix of herbaceous perennials, annuals and bulbs ensure an almost constant show of flowers through the seasons. Gaura (*Oenothera lindheimeri*), bloody cranesbill (*Geranium sanguineum*), red valerian (*Centranthus ruber*), brown-eyed susan (*Rudbeckia triloba*), garden cosmos (*Cosmos bipinnatus*), signet marigold (*Tagetes tenuifolia*), garden nasturtium (*Tropaeolum majus*) and red spider zinnia (*Zinnia tenuifolia*) create a rainbow of yellows, pinks, oranges, reds and purples.

Inside the pavilion is a space to house the owner's gardening tools, a simple kitchen made of galvanised steel and an area for entertaining. Liberal use of glass and large sliding doors allow a view across the garden to the alps. During summer the vines ensure the interior remains relatively cool; in winter – once the deciduous species have lost their leaves – more light flows inside, keeping the building comfortable throughout the year. This building both gives back to and is revitalised by nature.

Autumn House

CARLTON NORTH, VICTORIA, AUSTRALIA
COMPLETED 2021

Traditional Owners: Wurundjeri Woi-wurrung people of the Kulin Nation

PHOTOGRAPHY
Rory Gardiner

ARCHITECT
Studio Bright

LANDSCAPE ARCHITECT/ DESIGNER
Eckersley Garden Architecture

BUILDER
ProvanBuilt

From the street, Autumn House in Melbourne's inner north is as much tree as it is building, thanks to the mature elm (*Ulmus* sp.) that provides a striking green contrast to the surrounding laneways. The site is enclosed by a solid brick wall that wraps carefully around the large tree, giving the sense that a secret garden lies beyond. The angled mesh balanced along the top of the wall offers a modern framework for a myriad of plants that tempt passers-by with their fragrance and verdancy.

Right A study nook leads to the garden. **Below** A fiddle leaf fig and cardboard plant make a perfect pair indoors. **Opposite** Creeping rosemary and star jasmine cascade through the mesh structure. **Previous spread** Deciduous trees put on an autumn show for the occupants and their neighbours.

Above Timber and glass are punctuated by pops of green and pink. **Opposite** The kitchen and dining room open onto the lush internal courtyard that was built around a mature elm tree.

Right (top) The Victorian terrace has been sensitively restored and the new addition brings a whole new dimension to the home. **Right (bottom)** Curves are a common feature inside and out. **Opposite** Eventually the climbing plants will cover almost all of the mesh structure, making a beautiful contribution to the streetscape.

Negotiating the confluence of an original Victorian terrace, a 1980s renovation by architect Mick Jörgensen and the large elm, Studio Bright's extension adds a new layer that beautifully blends the house with its garden. Melissa Bright explains that Studio Bright looks for 'an opportunity in all projects to enhance the connection between people and their environment'. In the case of Autumn House, she says the design 'negotiates the need for refuge, retreat and privacy in its urban context while also adding to shared local greenery'.

In many ways, the design for this renovation is a direct response to the tree. The decision was made early on to preserve this important natural element and, while it certainly imposed constraints on what could be achieved, Melissa says that 'everyone could see the value in retaining an established tree in a dense urban environment and the benefit that it would bring to the owners as well as the neighbourhood'. The plan of the house extends outwards from the elm, 'surrounding and embracing the canopy and bringing the seasonal beauty of the tree into daily life'.

There is a wonderful fluidity between the interior and exterior spaces of Autumn House, achieved by the use of 'porous thresholds' that allow the downstairs living spaces to connect directly with the courtyard garden. This inner courtyard is at the heart of the home and plays a pivotal role in bringing natural light into the interior spaces. Architecture and landscape design work together harmoniously to elevate the lives of the young family who now live here.

Below The mesh structure provides privacy for the bedroom and supports climbing plants. **Opposite** Potted plants, a slim raised garden bed and mature tree canopies make for a verdant balcony. **Following spread** The restored brick floors and walls of the original home complement the concrete and timber of the new extension.

While the lower level of the house is dominated by brick and timber, the upper level is encased in a mesh structure in a rich hue that references the surrounding red-brick buildings. This mesh allows the house, when viewed from afar, to blend with its neighbours. On closer inspection, the perforations lighten the aesthetic of the structure and support climbing and cascading plants like star jasmine (*Trachelospermum jasminoides*) and creeping rosemary (*Rosmarinus officinalis* 'Prostratus'), creating a slim garden around the perimeter of the upper level that houses the main bedroom, ensuite and a rooftop deck. The screen, with its growing cover of greenery, filters light into the interiors and provides some privacy. But more than that it provides 'immersion in the immediate landscape and canopy of the elm tree'.

The hope is that, over time, the mesh structure will become completely engulfed in vegetation and 'become almost like a fragrant hedge sitting atop the brick base – an unexpected gift to the neighbourhood and lane'. Green spaces benefit owners and neighbours alike, and Autumn House exemplifies that – it is both a joy for the family who inhabits it and a gift to the street on which it sits.

[The] extension adds a new layer that beautifully blends the house with its garden.

House for a Garden

LILYFIELD, NEW SOUTH WALES, AUSTRALIA
COMPLETED 2017

Traditional Owners: Gadigal and Wangal peoples of the Eora Nation

PHOTOGRAPHY
Ben Hosking (interiors) and Clinton Weaver (garden)

Above The single-wall, birch plywood kitchen leads to the lounge room and backyard. **Opposite** Brick reclaimed from the original backyard paves an entertaining area that is shaded by a mature bottle brush. **Previous spread** The internal courtyard is now home to an olive tree of personal significance to the owner, along with a selection of herbs for use in the adjacent kitchen.

In the inner city, homes tend to be stacked neatly beside one another and have shared walls, or just a slim path between them. Limited (or, in some cases, no) natural light can penetrate these old buildings, resulting in dark and damp abodes. Modern renovations often include the addition of an internal courtyard that allows light and air to flow through. This simple design idea can make a world of difference to the liveability of a home, and when done right, allows its inhabitants a daily chance to engage with nature.

ARCHITECT
Retallack Thompson Architects

LANDSCAPE ARCHITECT
Kirsty Kendall (Studio Rewild)

BUILDER
Joseph McCombie Carpentry

Above left Meadow grass, vanilla lily and oak leaf kalanchoe create a welcoming front garden and attract native birds and bees. **Above right** Creeping rosemary cascades over the edge of the courtyard garden. **Opposite** Placing the courtyard in the heart of the home gives the dining area, kitchen and lounge room a direct connection to the garden.

Sydney architects Jemima Retallack and Mitchell Thompson – partners in life and work – have created a unique and meaningful take on this idea with their Lilyfield project, created for Jemima's mother, Bridget. The brief was to modernise the existing bungalow by building a functional and comfortable single-storey home that Bridget could grow old in while creating a greater connection to nature within the space.

The design approach was simple: 'Less house, more garden.' They did this by adding a meagre 4 square metres (43 square feet) internally and ensuring a constant connection to the outdoors and plants throughout the home. The neutral internal palette of soft greys, whites, birch plywood joinery and cypress pine flooring also aids by drawing the eye to the newly added or invigorated green spaces.

Landscape architect Kirsty Kendall of Studio Rewild always starts by considering an indigenous plant palette and soil type, ensuring the ecology of the site is at the forefront of design decisions. 'Incorporating a diversity of species – a rich plant palette with the local endemic species as the starting point – is imperative at this juncture. As landscape architects and garden designers, we have a responsibility to create gardens, no matter how big or small, that contribute to habitat value. [This is] especially critical in urban spaces where habitats are dwindling.' At the front of the building, meadow grasses (*Poa* spp.), oak leaf kalanchoe (*Kalanchoe beharensis* 'Oak leaf') and vanilla lily (*Arthropodium milleflorum*) create a soft, joyful and floriferous welcome and provide food and a resting place for native birds and the much-revered blue-banded bee (*Amegilla cingulata*). Towards the rear of the property, brick reclaimed from the

Light and air flow into the home through the internal courtyard, tempered by a stainless steel chainmail curtain.

original backyard provides paving for entertaining, while the neighbour's avocado tree (*Persea americana*) and Bridget's mature bottlebrush (*Callistemon* sp.) provide a shaded canopy that is complemented by the dark greens of the native chef's cap correa (*Correa baeuerlenii*), bolwarra (*Eupomatia laurina*) and edible apple berry (*Billardiera scandens*).

But the real hero of this home is the courtyard to which the new living areas are oriented. This green space is a productive zone, providing herbs for the adjacent kitchen, and a bounty of light and ventilation for the entire rear of the property. At its centre stands a 20-year-old olive tree (*Olea europaea*), which had grown in a large pot at Bridget's previous homes. Planting this tree in the ground was a significant moment, one of homecoming, of finding place and fulfilling Bridget's dream of having a home with a garden to tend and enjoy. Kirsty says, 'The olive became the fulcrum of the courtyard and set the tone for the herbaceous silvery grey plantings in this area.'

This home is a perfect example of doing more with less. And it proves that you don't need a huge property to allow nature to be adeptly designed into a space.

Merrick's Farmhouse

MORNINGTON PENINSULA, VICTORIA, AUSTRALIA
COMPLETED 2021

Traditional Owners: Bunurong/Boon Wurrung people of the Kulin Nation

PHOTOGRAPHY
Tom Ross

ARCHITECT
Michael Lumby Architecture in collaboration with Nielsen Jenkins

LANDSCAPE DESIGNERS
Franchesca Watson and Robyn Barlow

BUILDER
Atma Builders

An elegant reimagining of the quintessential Australian farmhouse, this inspired hilltop home enjoys spectacular views across grassy paddocks to the rugged coast of Victoria's Mornington Peninsula. South African–based Michael Lumby Architecture, working with Nielsen Jenkins in Brisbane, have created a family home that feels truly connected to its bucolic setting.

Right HAY Palissade dining armchairs pair perfectly with an inbuilt concrete table. **Below** View from the internal courtyard through the home to the surrounding landscape. **Opposite** Water is featured heavily, from the pond to the large, round water tanks. **Previous spread** The monolithic nature of the building is softened by layered and contrasting planting, including burgundy willow myrtle and blue-purple morning iris.

The clients, a couple relocating from Melbourne, required an adaptable space that would accommodate the two of them for most of the year but also allow them to host larger gatherings of friends and family for holidays and celebrations. This generously proportioned house is cleverly designed so that much of the space can be closed off when not needed, with the front wing of the house functioning as an intimate one-bedroom pavilion.

In response to the exposed site that needed protection from sometimes extreme weather, a robust materials palette was selected. Thick concrete block walls extend outwards from the building's interior, framing views to the greenery and guiding movement through the home. Planting along the walls softens the building, balancing the monolithic aesthetic and allowing it to blend with its surroundings. With its generous low-lying roof and deep overhangs, the house feels beautifully grounded – it is almost an extension of the landscape.

The roof also captures rainwater, which is stored in large tanks for eventual reuse. Rather than concealing the tanks, the architects celebrated these ubiquitous pieces of farming paraphernalia – circular containers are a motif that appear throughout the project in the form of birdbaths, ponds and a fire pit.

Where possible, the existing planting informed the design decisions. An avenue of elms (*Ulmus* sp.) that lined the original driveway was retained to form the main pedestrian entry and a windbreak of lilly pillies (*Syzygium* sp.) north of the new pool was also preserved.

In an *ArchDaily* profile, the architects explain that 'the architecture recedes and the building acts simply as a lens from which to experience the landscape'. The plan of the single-level dwelling is centred around an impressive central courtyard, an outdoor space that is in many ways the most important room in the house. Sheltered and introspective, it provides a lush focal point and refuge from the expansive surrounds of the property.

An avenue of mature elms forms the main pedestrian entryway. Many of the thick concrete block walls are topped with blue chalksticks.

Above Dark timber and concrete features throughout the interiors reinforce the feeling of refuge and shelter. **Opposite** The sunken lounge room looks onto the lush internal courtyard and enjoys additional light from a long, narrow skylight that punctures the dark ceiling.

The landscaping of the central courtyard by South African garden designer Franchesca Watson and Australian landscape architect and horticulturalist Robyn Barlow is ethereal and textured. Both designers are passionate about creating truly sustainable gardens, so plants were selected that suited the climate of the site, the lifestyle of the clients and the architecture. The slim dark leaves of the West Australian willow myrtle cultivars (*Agonis flexuosa* 'Burgundy' and 'After Dark') are the heroes of this garden, softening the architecture and pulling the eye up. Boston ivy (*Parthenocissus tricuspidata*) suckers its way up the concrete block walls, some of which are topped with glaucous blue chalksticks (*Senecio serpens*). Throughout the garden are swathes of native plants, such as fern-like banksia (*Banksia blechnifolia*), purple-flowering morning flag (*Orthrosanthus multiflorus*) and digger's speedwell (*Veronica perfoliata*), as well as yellow paper daisy (*Xerochrysum viscosum*). Combined with a diverse selection of grasses – kangaroo grass (*Themeda triandra*) and leatherleaf sedge (*Carex buchananii*) along with tassel cord rush (*Baloskion tetraphyllum* syn. *Restio tetraphyllus*) in the ponds – the planting of soft and contrasting species creates an elegantly layered landscape.

Arranging the interior spaces as a series of blocks around this and other outdoor spaces, including the calming pool terrace and more intimate gardens adjoining the bedrooms, ensures glimpses to nature from every room. Outward views to the surrounding landscape are also maximised by floor-to-ceiling glazing. The result is a house that is truly embedded in nature.

[The architects] have created a family home that feels truly connected to its bucolic setting.

Below The swimming pool is bordered with copper-coloured leatherleaf sedge. **Opposite** The internal courtyard backs onto the double-height library. **Previous spread (clockwise from top left)** From a distance, the house looks like a traditional farmhouse. // View from the master en suite to the adjoining courtyard – nature is never far away. // The circular water tank motif continues throughout the landscaping.

House in Kyoto

KYOTO, JAPAN
COMPLETED 2019

PHOTOGRAPHY
Yosuke Ohtake

Above Hinoki cypress is used for the floors, ceilings, stairs and screening. **Opposite** A green mosaic mural gives the bathroom a luxurious, forest feel. **Previous spread** This weeping fig was chosen for its attractive drooping leaves and its ability to thrive indoors.

For his first foray into designing a house from scratch, architect Joe Chikamori of 07BEACH has created a beautifully functional family home with plants at its core. Located on a narrow road in a quiet residential area in northern Kyoto, House in Kyoto is flanked on three sides by houses that extend to the site's boundaries. This is an area pretty much devoid of green space for outdoor play – not ideal for a family with three young children. From the initial discussions with the clients, the inclusion of a garden was a main consideration, along with an open-plan layout that would allow the parents sightlines to the children throughout the house.

ARCHITECT
07BEACH

LANDSCAPE DESIGNER
07BEACH

BUILDER
Kyuma Sekkei Komu

Above The weeping fig has become another member of the family. **Opposite** Traditional Japanese movable screens and doors are used to open the rooms onto the central atrium.

It became clear that the typical layout of a house with a garden at the rear wasn't going to offer an attractive outdoor area or be the best use of space, so the architects explored alternative layouts around the idea of a central courtyard. Initial designs incorporated a glassed internal space that was open to the sky, but this interrupted the flow of the house. By removing the glass and opting for skylights to fill the inner living space with natural light, they were able to integrate the garden inside while maintaining the openness of the home. Essentially, Joe explains, 'the idea of a large central atrium with a family-like tree growing in the middle was a good fit for everyone'.

Timber – the culturally significant Hinoki cypress – features heavily throughout, in floors, ceilings, stairs and screening. In the pursuit of a singular interior space, there are few internal walls – slatted timber screens provide flexible partitioning. Even the bathroom opens completely to the main living space, apart from a curtain screen that is rarely used, with the bathtub offering views to the tree for a feeling of 'open-air bathing'. An impressive green mosaic mural on the bathroom wall, the handiwork of a local craftsman, references a forest scene, further introducing nature inside.

It is in the central, double-height living space that House in Kyoto beautifully resolves how to bring the outside in. With little opportunity for the inclusion of windows on the building's facades, large skylights in the sloped roof bring daylight flooding into the space from which all the rooms in the house extend. The tree growing in this room is poetically seen as another member of the family. The tree will grow as the three children do, strengthening the family's relationship to the house, each other and nature as a whole. Although choosing a species that would best suit the indoor conditions was a challenge, a consultation with an experienced indoor tree specialist helped them settle on a weeping fig (*Ficus benjamina*). This is an evergreen tree with dainty drooping foliage that can thrive indoors.

House in Kyoto offers a creative and elegant solution for urban living that successfully explores the notion of connection to nature by cleverly responding to the constraints of its site and the needs and desires of the client. It shows that, even in the most subtle of ways, plants can positively impact a home and the day-to-day lives of the people who inhabit it.

This clever layout creates a double-height living space in the centre of the home. Multiple skylights allow lots of natural light into the home and there is plenty of space for the internal tree to grow into over time.

Ground House
107R

TINTENBAR, NEW SOUTH WALES, AUSTRALIA
COMPLETED 2022

Traditional Owners: Nyangbul people of the Bundjalung Nation

PHOTOGRAPHY
Bec Willox

ARCHITECT
David Fewson

LANDSCAPE DESIGNERS
LARC Landscape Architecture and Nicholas Ward Landscapes (now Taylor & Ward Landscapes)

BUILDER
David Fewson

Designed to be the second guesthouse on a sprawling property in Tintenbar, on the far north coast of New South Wales, Ground House 107R is the handiwork of local craftsman and builder David Fewson and his creative family. It sits alongside the Fewson's original family home and their self-contained guesthouse, Paddock Hall.

Right and below Soft curtains diffuse the light and their sheer quality encourages guests to rise with the sun. **Opposite** Creeping rosemary, pigface and flowering aloe thrive on the exposed rooftop garden. **Previous spread** Despite its brutalist aesthetic, the house's placement in a natural amphitheatre with generous landscaping helps it blend into the surrounding landscape.

Left Wood and brass feature heavily and were chosen for the beautiful way they wear and age. **Opposite** The owner-builder worked with local artisans, including a brass fabricator who created the bespoke splashbacks and countertops in the kitchen.

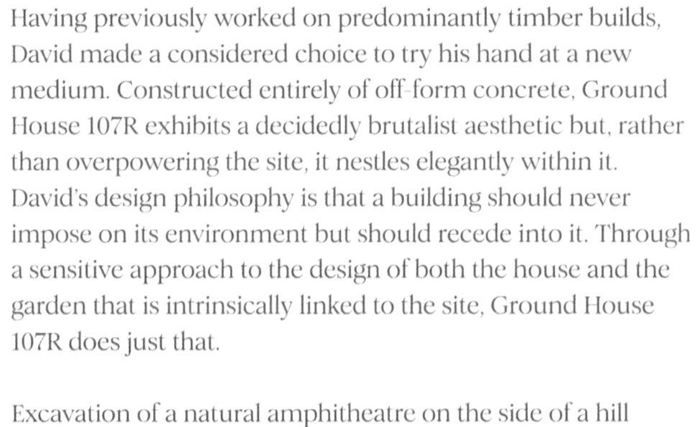

Having previously worked on predominantly timber builds, David made a considered choice to try his hand at a new medium. Constructed entirely of off-form concrete, Ground House 107R exhibits a decidedly brutalist aesthetic but, rather than overpowering the site, it nestles elegantly within it. David's design philosophy is that a building should never impose on its environment but should recede into it. Through a sensitive approach to the design of both the house and the garden that is intrinsically linked to the site, Ground House 107R does just that.

Excavation of a natural amphitheatre on the side of a hill ensured the silhouette of the site's topography was not altered and allowed the building to embed itself into the landscape. David's daughter Hannah, who now manages the property, describes it as being like 'a spacecraft that crash-landed into the side of the hill . . . creating a rolling "wake" of earth as it skidded to a halt'.

Beginning with the roof garden, the architecture reads as a continuation of the landscape, while the planting reflects the phenomenon of vegetation reclaiming an abandoned site. The building appears fully settled in its surroundings, almost as though it has always been there.

The Fewsons worked closely with Luke Jones from LARC Landscape Architecture to achieve the building's green roof. This was no mean feat, given the extensive concrete span, free from supporting pillars, and the weight of earth it was required to hold. Sealing, engineering and drainage were all important elements to get right.

Above The house was designed to resemble a spacecraft that has crashed to Earth and embedded itself in the hill.
Following spread Touches of deep red, both internally and externally, add warmth and richness.

Working with 'the loose brief that the roof needed to look like a naturally occurring vegetative swathe in the existing landscape', David's green-thumbed wife, Jane, worked with landscaper Nicholas Ward to 'choose native ground covers, vines and succulents that could tolerate the full sun and that would grow to provide a nice variety of heights and drapery'. Native pigface (*Carpobrotus glaucescens*), creeping rosemary (*Rosmarinus officinalis* 'Prostratus'), flowering aloe (*Aloe* sp.) and grasses such as lomandra mist (*Lomandra confertifolia* ssp. *rubiginosa* 'Mist') and Mascarene grass (*Zoysia tenuifolia*) are thriving on the exposed roof. In the sunken courtyard, sun-loving creeping thyme (*Thymus serpyllum*) and clumping native grasses were selected for their ability to tolerate the hot conditions.

Ground House 107R's expansive glass facades unite the interiors with the outside, allowing natural light to flood the space and providing unencumbered views to the surrounding greenery. Opening the compact interior to its surroundings effectively creates an increased sense of space. As a home specifically built for short-term guests, the design allows the occupants to become fully immersed in the natural beauty of the site for the short time they are there. Sheer curtains encourage waking with the sun and facilitate the experience of the many moods of the space as the light shifts through the surrounding bush.

Beginning with the roof garden, the architecture reads as a continuation of the landscape.

A warm and tactile palette of materials, including timber, brass and jade, pair perfectly with the colours and textures of the landscape. David's vision for a simple but highly crafted interior was executed in collaboration with Jane and Hannah. The cabinetry in the bathroom and kitchen, along with the floating bed, were all designed by David and built by him with the help of a local friend and cabinet-maker. Each concave strip of timber that makes up the cabinetry facing was finished by hand. Hannah explains that the extensive use of brass throughout the space, from the tapware, and countertops to the bespoke light fittings, 'was informed by a longstanding love David has for the material and its aesthetic dynamism. Its "alive" nature and the way it tarnishes and reacts to contact with different products and foods.' All these materials work in harmony to bring softness to the space.

Ground House 107R shows what can be achieved with a curious and creative mind. It is a testament to both craftsmanship and working with, rather than against, an existing landscape.

Rosenlund Naturhus

VADSTENA, SWEDEN
COMPLETED 2021

PHOTOGRAPHY
Karin Wildheim

ARCHITECT
Fredrik Olson

LANDSCAPE DESIGNER
Client

BUILDER
Client

In response to the cold Nordic winters, and with the important goal of creating a more sustainable way of living, Swedish architect Bengt Warne developed the first prototype of his Naturhus (nature house) in the 1970s. More recently, the concept has been popularised by ecocycle system and greenhouse technology expert Anders Solvarm. Anders, along with architect and building engineer Fredrik Olson, Niklas Dahlström and Dan-Eric Archer, went on to co-found Greenhouse Living, a company made up of an interdisciplinary team of consultants who develop, design and help to build naturhus.

Right Nasturtium creeps from the garden bed into the indoor/outdoor area between the internal corehouse and the protective outer greenhouse. **Below** The greenhouse has a vast array of plants that could not grow in the harsh Nordic climate. **Opposite** The naturhus concept involves placing a traditional house in a glass enclosure, resulting in a very non-traditional home. **Previous spread** A closed system transforms waste into nutrient-dense fertiliser for the plants, which in turn nourish the occupants.

C24 M 0402 EKSJÖ INDUSTRI AB
DRY GRADED 07 W104

Right Agave, fruit trees, tomatoes and grapes grow in abundance. **Opposite** The owners grow much of their food in the temperate Mediterranean microclimate of the greenhouse. **Previous spread** In the greenhouse, the boundary between outside and inside is blurred.

At its core, the Naturhus concept consists of a greenhouse, a core house and an ecocycle system. The external glazed greenhouse often has plenty of solar panelling, and the internal, natural material heavy core house can be either an existing building or one purpose built for the project. The productive ecocycle system works by creating a closed loop: collecting grey water to be recycled and transforming sewage waste into nutrient-rich fertiliser for the gardens.

A deep reverence for nature is ingrained in Swedish culture, and the naturhus style of living integrates nature into every aspect of life. Light floods in through the greenhouse walls and ceiling, automated hatches open when cooling and ventilation is required, large windows and doors invite the occupants into the protected zone between home and greenhouse, and plants tumble into this area from gardens and raised beds.

In the design and build of Rosenlund Naturhus, Fredrik and the Greenhouse Living team collaborated closely with owners Roja Brimalm and Johan Holmstedt, a chef and mechanic. Incredibly, Johan and Roja, more or less on their own, assembled almost all of the greenhouse structure and have been busy creating an abundant garden in the relatively temperate Mediterranean microclimate created by the glasshouse. Along with ornamentals like dahlia (*Dahlia* spp.) and agave (*Agave* spp.), Roja and Johan grow a stunning variety of edibles not generally found in colder climates, such as fig (*Ficus carica*), melon (*Cucumis* spp.), grape (*Vitis* spp.), olive (*Olea europaea*), mango (*Mangifera indica*) and watermelon (*Citrullus lanatus*).

Fredrik describes the vision of the Naturhus as 'a sustainable building that produces food, instead of waste. A house that generates energy instead of just consuming it . . . What you flush down comes back to your own ecocycle system and into the tomatoes you give your children to eat. A sustainable architecture that promotes a truly sustainable lifestyle.'

Redfern House

REDFERN, NEW SOUTH WALES, AUSTRALIA
COMPLETED 2023

Traditional Owners: Gadigal people of the Eora Nation

PHOTOGRAPHY
Clinton Weaver

Above View through the new studio towards the main house. **Opposite** From the new living space, the tropical courtyard is framed by a large window and glazed door. **Previous spread** Skylights in the new extension draw light into this inner-city residence.

Architect Anthony Gill has a special ability to transform small, dark inner-city residences into lush, light-filled homes. His conceptualisation of space means that every inch is thoughtfully considered, planned and programmed in a way that feels discreet and luxurious at the same time. Anthony explains that 'at every opportunity, we try to link the spaces strongly with the garden'. This interplay between the outdoor and indoor areas enhances the feeling of spaciousness of both.

ARCHITECT
Anthony Gill Architects

LANDSCAPE ARCHITECT
Sacha Coles

BUILDER
Castle Construction

Left (top) Timber walls and floors in the studio space. **Left (bottom)** Stainless steel benchtops and timber joinery in the kitchen. **Opposite** Timber batten screens have become a calling card for architect Anthony Gill.

Redfern House, designed in collaboration with the owner, landscape architect Sacha Coles, was always going to hold landscape at the core of its design. The narrow terrace, spanning four floors (including a below-ground level), was transformed from a two-bedroom home to one with four bedrooms. A new living area replaced an old lean-to, and a two-storey studio built off the rear lane houses a studio, laundry and storage for the family's bikes. Above the new living area sits a verdant rooftop garden and between the two buildings is a lush courtyard. These two green spaces are at the heart of the design.

The rooftop garden, which is visible from the main house and the studio, anchors this home. Sacha says it 'was always considered as the centrepiece of the project'. It provides a sense of calm, not only for the occupants, but also for their neighbours. Sacha has planted a combination of natives and exotics, leading to a garden that is not just maintenance-free but 'buzzing with native bees and other insects'. Shade-tolerant spur flower (*Plectranthus* spp.) and happy wanderer (*Hardenbergia* spp.) were planted at the foot of the fences at the north of the block. Sun-tolerant species, such as pineapple sage (*Salvia elegans*), fountain grass (*Pennisetum* spp.) and knotted club-rush (*Ficinia nodosa*), are planted along the opposite side. Three circular skylights built into the roof, which resemble tranquil pools of water when viewed in the context of the garden, allow light to flood into the living spaces below. Both the living spaces and roof garden are complemented by the courtyard. Receiving a limited amount of direct sun, it has a more tropical feel, and is filled abundantly with palms, figs and ferns, including a giant mounted elkhorn fern (*Platycerium bifurcatum*).

Including heavily planted gardens in the design is important to Anthony's practice. He believes that involving landscape architects and designers early in the design process is crucial to the successful marriage of the landscaping and the architecture. '[By] dedicating as much outdoor space as possible to a densely planted garden . . . as opposed to a lawn or hard surfaces, the overall experience is significantly enriched.'

Below Timber venetian blinds cover the windows of the main house. **Opposite** Fountain grass, knotted club-rush and red flowering pineapple sage are just a few of the plants in the beautifully wild and low-maintenance roof garden.

Sense of Self Bathhouse

COLLINGWOOD, VICTORIA, AUSTRALIA
COMPLETED 2021

Traditional Owners: Wurundjeri Woi-wurrung people of the Kulin Nation

PHOTOGRAPHY
Martina Gemmola

ARCHITECTS
Setsquare Studio, Chamberlain Architecture & Interiors and Hearth Studio

INTERIOR DESIGNER
Setsquare Studio

LANDSCAPE DESIGNER
Ryan Klewer

BUILDER
MIC Projects

A truly collaborative project, Sense of Self Bathhouse in Melbourne is a space that exudes relaxation and restoration. The design team, led by Caitlin Perry of Setsquare Studio alongside Sarah Trotter from Hearth Studio and Ella Leoncio from Chamberlain Architecture & Interiors, worked with the visionaries behind Sense Of Self to create a bathhouse that goes far beyond your standard wellness offering.

Right Japanese aralia, Swiss cheese plant and philodendron xanadu thrive in the humid conditions of the bathhouse. **Below** A shower area for guests to cleanse and cool down. **Opposite** Water and plants are revered for their healing qualities. **Previous spread** A tree fern and an umbrella tree are potted in aged terracotta vessels while Tahitian bridal veil and various succulents and cacti trail from hanging planters.

Left (top) A Circa Curved Floormount Mixer tap by Sussex is paired with a textured sink. **Left (bottom)** Nooks for resting are found throughout the space. **Opposite (and following spread)** Light floods into the former warehouse through its large windows.

Occupying a converted double-storey brick warehouse in fashionable Collingwood, Sense Of Self incorporates a large mineral bath, Finnish sauna, cold plunge, hammam (Turkish bath) and day spa and also has plenty of space for contemplation and slowing down. The founders' personal connections to the Mediterranean and Norway informed much of the look and feel of the interiors.

Setting out to provide a truly immersive experience, Caitlin and Ella explain that the bathhouse's guests are invited to 'better connect with themselves and their immediate physical world'. Unsurprisingly, natural elements play an active role. 'The design team were interested in the idea of bathing as a sort of reverence to water – a deep appreciation for the way it moves, the way it can be a driver for growth and the way it can provide healing and nourishment.'

An exploration of erosion, reflectivity and patina had a strong influence on the material palette. Beautifully strong and textured concrete, travertine, micro-cement and sandstone boulders are used throughout in a way that encourages them to wear and age as they would in the natural environment. Water references are reflected in the use of mineral colours and metals such as aged brass. Deep greens and terracotta tones add to a palette that aligns perfectly with a Mediterranean aesthetic.

Plants were seen as a key inclusion from the outset, 'not just for their aesthetic properties but rather tapping into their deeper sense of "wellbeing"', explains Caitlin. Landscape designer Ryan Klewer initially reached out to the founders of Sense of Self via Instagram after observing the construction as a passer-by – and thus, another creative collaboration was born. On learning that the space was going to be a bathhouse, Ryan envisaged 'a lush and verdant oasis reminiscent of the legendary Hanging Gardens of Babylon'.

The selection and placement of the plants was designed to encourage interactions between the guests and their surroundings, providing 'moments of seclusion behind lush foliage or fostering a sense of communal comfort through strategically placed vines'. Diverse environmental conditions within the space also had a major influence on the final design. The different bathhouse zones each had unique requirements – as is often the case with gardening, a process of trial and error led to the final selection.

With a shared vision and a relatively open brief, Ryan decided on a mix of ground-based pot plants in a variety of scales and suspended hanging baskets and vines, reminiscent of Ancient Roman bathhouses. Ornate terracotta, weathered by time and adorned with intricate textures, showcase an array of carefully chosen plant species. Larger specimens, including a seriously impressive mature staghorn fern (*Platycerium superbum*) that majestically welcomes guests when they first arrive, and other tropical plants like umbrella fig (*Ficus umbellata*), philodendrons such as Congo rojo (*Philodendron tatei* ssp. *Melanochlorum*), umbrella plant (*Schefflera* spp.), tree ferns and Swiss cheese plant (*Monstera deliciosa*), provide points of focus as well as foliage for privacy. Hanging baskets of Tahitian bridal veil (*Gibasis pellucida*) and heart leaf philodendron (*Philodendron cordatum*) add height variation, particularly in the double-height courtyard area, and the trailing vines screen and obscure views through the space.

At Sense of Self, elements of the natural world have been triumphantly incorporated to create a restorative wellness experience. It is a space in which the living aspect brings calm, softness and nourishment that is beneficial for body and mind.

An exploration of erosion, reflectivity and patina had a strong influence on the material palette.

Above A diverse selection of indoor plants gently guide you through the space. **Opposite** A mature staghorn fern greets guests on arrival. **Previous spread** Highly textured materials, such as travertine, micro-cement and sandstone, sit alongside terracotta and aged brass to create a warm and welcoming environment.

Garden House

WESTERN PORT BAY, VICTORIA, AUSTRALIA
COMPLETED 2013 – ONGOING

Traditional Owners: Bunurong/Boon Wurrung people of the Kulin Nation

PHOTOGRAPHY
Rory Gardiner

Above and opposite Carefully regenerated native vegetation springs up between the raised platform of the building and its polycarbonate shell. **Previous spread** As the vegetation grows, the building – part-shed, part-tent – recedes further into the landscape.

From its coastal position on Victoria's Western Port Bay, Garden House merges into a bushy landscape of regenerated vegetation. The 'sometimes' house of architects and owners Mauro Baracco and Louise Wright, this building is a beautifully minimal architectural expression, stripped back to the barest of essentials. Open-plan living areas, including a simple kitchen and dining space, an open mezzanine sleeping quarter and an enclosed bathroom, sit on a raised deck and platform that is ensconced in a transparent shell of polycarbonate cladding. Nature is ever-present both inside and out.

ARCHITECT
Baracco+Wright Architects

LANDSCAPE ARCHITECT/ DESIGNER
Baracco+Wright Architects

BUILDER
Melbourne Garages

Right (top) The raised platform minimises disturbance to the ground below and allows floodwater to flow underneath, protecting the structure from damage. **Right (bottom)** The minimal kitchen is low-fi but functional. **Opposite** A wood-burning fire in the open-plan living space provides much-needed warmth on cooler nights.

As in previous projects, Mauro and Louise further their exploration of the concept of the tent. Doing away with many of the conventions of what constitutes a standard house, such as solid walls and flooring, simulates the experience of camping. The permeable structure facilitates a complete immersion in nature for the occupants. A connection to the landscape is felt on many levels, from unfettered access to natural light and ventilation through to a full sensory experience of external sounds. Exposure to the temperate climate of south-eastern Victoria is – for the most part – comfortable, but the architects certainly don't shy away from experiencing the hotter days or cooler nights of the region.

All design decisions for Garden House stemmed from a desire to create something simple and low impact that would simultaneously enable the regeneration and embrace the indigenous habitat around it. Louise observes that 'architecture, or say urbanity, is responsible for displacing the environment'. She advocates for a meaningful approach to integrating or connecting architecture with nature – one that makes 'actual space and deep soil for an ecosystem to connect, remain, restore and function . . . sometimes that means not building in certain places, or carefully designing to get out of the way'.

Above A mezzanine level constructed of plywood houses the bedroom, which is a perfect spot to listen to local wildlife or the patter of rain. **Opposite** The polycarbonate shell is punctured by sliding walls on two sides. Inside, the ground is completely unsealed, allowing a garden to grow around the raised structure.

5024AGS X 5352mm #0005319812_618

The architect-owners have a relationship with the landscape that goes well beyond the aesthetic. They have fully embraced a building that welcomes the local plants, wildlife and climate into its confines.

The building itself is almost secondary to the significance of the natural landscape. The project began with works to regenerate the land. Remnant vegetation was identified and weeding commenced outwards from those areas (known as the Bradley Method). The eventual footprint of the building was selected as an area on the site where the vegetation failed to thrive, most likely because of landfill underneath. The house plays a vital role in the rejuvenation of the flora within the area. Louise explains that the see-through shell 'provides the thinnest of physical boundaries'. In conjunction with the floor, which has been raised to allow the flow of floodwater common in the area, this creates a 'framework to be colonised by vegetation over time, both inside and out'.

A symbiotic relationship exists between the structure and the surrounding vegetation. The ground of the house is predominantly unsealed, encouraging plant growth within the confines of the house. These plants shade and cool the space. Endemic species, such as swamp gum (*Eucalyptus ovata*), black she-oak (*Allocasuarina littoralis*) and the charming greenhood orchid (*Pterostylis nutans*), will thrive and be enjoyed for generations of humans and wildlife to come. Thanks to the careful and considered work of Louise and Mauro and their reverence for nature, Garden House has become a key part of a thriving ecosystem.

Sunday

FITZROY, VICTORIA, AUSTRALIA
COMPLETED 2022

Traditional Owners: Wurundjeri Woi-wurrung people of the Kulin Nation

PHOTOGRAPHY
Tom Ross

ARCHITECT
Architecture architecture

LANDSCAPE ARCHITECT/ DESIGNER
Amanda Oliver Gardens

BUILDER
Grenville Architectural Constructions

Described by architect Michael Roper as 'a home for physical and psychological wellbeing, providing a diversity of spaces where occupants can always find a place of comfort', Sunday is a sanctuary in inner-city Melbourne. Having occupied the modest-sized house for some time in its original state, the owners set out to rework it, not to increase its size but to make the space more optimal for living. Their goal was 'better, not bigger'. Steering clear of the typical plan for a terrace dwelling and responding instead to a brief from the owners that focused more on creating their desired atmosphere and living experience, the architects effectively explored what it really means to live well.

Right Light streams into the kitchen through the fluted-glass clerestory windows. **Below** Breeze blocks feature extensively throughout the home, simultaneously revealing and concealing. **Opposite** The planting in the courtyard is textural and layered, softening the robust material palette. **Previous spread** The yellow sunken lounge looks out to the lush central courtyard.

Above left Creepers like this fine-leaved Boston ivy will grow up to the timber beams as they mature. **Above right** Building to the back of the block maximises the floorplan. **Opposite** The yellow sunken bath is a tranquil spot surrounded by garden. **Previous spread** Retiring to the private realm through the open courtyard becomes a more considered and elevated experience.

Heritage requirements meant the existing street facade and front room had to be retained. Beyond that was a different story. The extension defies spatial constraints by using a chequered plan that first separates the space into three bands – communal, outdoor and private realms – then each of these spaces are divided to create both a generous and an intimate zone. The spaces shift from social at the front of the home to private towards the back.

The compact site – just 175 square metres (1884 square feet) – made it challenging to deliver meaningful outdoor space. The solution was a central courtyard. 'By building to the back of the block and having a full-width courtyard in the centre of the house, we effectively doubled the garden frontage, bringing natural light, ventilation and greenery into more of the house.' Not only is the courtyard a room unto itself, it provides views to greenery that can be enjoyed from both sides of the home, and adds privacy to the living spaces.

The importance of the courtyard cannot be understated. It makes movement through the home more intentional. 'Accessing the bedroom requires walking across the open-air courtyard, providing a deliberate retreat from the house – a valuable gesture on a site where separation of zones is challenging.' Retiring for the evening becomes a more considered ritual, while the full-width design gives the occupants a greater awareness of their environment. As Michael explains, they 'are more conscious of the weather, which plays a role in the daily experience of home life: wet weather requires a quick dash across the courtyard; warm weather permits the doors to be thrown open'. There is a sense of ceremony to life in this home, an elevation of everyday living.

The lush planting by Amanda Oliver Gardens is designed to extend upwards to the timber joists over time, thanks to the use of vining plants such as silver vein creeper (*Parthenocissus henryana*) and fine-leaved Boston ivy (*Parthenocissus tricuspidata* 'Lowii'). Mixed in with shrubs, including gold dust wattle (*Acacia acinacea*) and Chinese plumbago (*Ceratostigma willmottianum*), are ground covers of cut-leaved daisy (*Brachyscome multifida*) and native violet (*Viola hederacea*). The resulting garden is incredibly textural and gently softens the raw and robust concrete, timber and steel that dominate the materials palette.

The other materials used in this renovation are strong but muted, and have a sense of geometry at their core. Most notably, the extensive use of breeze blocks with their graphic punctuations exemplify the concept of separation and connection explored in the design. Along with the fluted north-facing clerestory windows, they beautifully sculpt the natural light entering the spaces and help to blur the distinction between inside and out. Throughout, natural textures are celebrated and juxtaposed, and the pops of yellow in the sunken lounge and bath are a nod to the owners' love of the work of Mexican architect Luis Barragán.

This house is a celebration of the ability of architecture to transform people's lives, using green space to elevate their daily activities and ensure this home is enjoyed to its full capacity.

The private area is separated from the living areas by the courtyard, reinforcing the sense of sanctuary.

PSLab London

LONDON, ENGLAND, UK
COMPLETED 2019

PHOTOGRAPHY
Rory Gardiner

ARCHITECT
JAMESPLUMB

LANDSCAPE DESIGNER
JAMESPLUMB

When lighting design company PSLab, headquartered in Beirut and with offices around the world, was looking to establish its London home, it sought out artists James Russell and Hannah Plumb of JAMESPLUMB. Having worked together on the design of an Aesop store in 2015, there was existing chemistry between the two creative teams, who share an appreciation for deeply considered objects and spaces.

Right Within the expansive warehouse space, smaller nooks are created by a series of concrete plinths that delineate spaces and function as seats, workspaces and planters. **Below** The open-plan layout incorporates a kitchen and a small auditorium. **Opposite** Plants grow from inbuilt planters and terracotta vessels, softening the brutalist aesthetic and providing areas that encourage creativity and collaboration. **Previous spread** Soft light filters through oversized windows.

PSLab
22 Wilds Rents
London SE1 4QG
www.pslab.net

Right (top) The entry courtyard showcases some of the building's original features and is a space to gather and enjoy the greenery. **Right (bottom)** Meeting rooms provide privacy in the otherwise open-plan headquarters. **Opposite** A verdant potted garden welcomes staff and visitors.

Aspiring to be more than simply a showroom or an office, the PSLab UK headquarters is a 'space to explore light and shadow', says Hannah. The design needed to foster creativity and collaboration and be flexible enough to accommodate changing day-to-day needs. A former late Victorian tannery in South London was chosen and the team set to work, stripping it back to its bones in order to create a new, thoughtful and highly emotive space.

Hannah and James, who are partners in life as well as work, met at art school and collaborated more informally before founding their eponymous studio in 2019. Their background in fine art and sculpture intersects with their interest in and keen eye for interiors and architectural design. As they succinctly put it, they 'make objects and create environments'. For PSLab's London home, as with their other projects, there was a rigorous research and planning process. Physical mock-ups allowed them to experiment with layout and materials and role play movement through the space.

Described by the designers as having a 'quiet brutalism', monumental slabs of concrete were employed to create an interior landscape within the warehouse shell. These slabs, along with changes in level, help to delineate spaces within the building and also function as furniture – a dining table, a sitting area and a shelf for plants. The new design is largely open plan and encompasses an atelier, kitchen, garden, dining room and library, along with meeting spaces and a small auditorium. The materials are all deeply considered. The concrete has been left intentionally imperfect, giving it a hand-hewn feeling, and hand-dyed linen, Lebanese glassware and timber are textural and inviting.

Gardens in the entry courtyard and the internal space play an important role in softening the brutalist feel and welcoming staff and clients to the space. The goal was to have greenery 'planted in the building' so it would feel 'a part of it. Committed.' This green space, like everything the team has created, is carefully thought through. It offers places to pause, to learn and to converse. Various figs (*Ficus* spp.), philodendron, Zanzibar gem (*Zamioculcas zamiifolia*), cast-iron plant (*Aspidistra elatior*), asparagus fern (*Asparagus* spp.) and the patterned never never plant (*Ctenanthe* spp.) offer an unexpected richness. Plants potted into terracotta vessels and antique metal tubs are interspersed throughout the space, sitting beside those growing from the inbuilt planters. This interplay adds poeticism and balance to the space.

This is a building that feels permanent. It is a sturdy base on which to create and play. One that is open to ideas, discovery, growth and understanding.

The former tannery was stripped back to its industrial shell, leaving just the original brickwork, steel pylons and pits that had once been used for dyeing. Although solid and permanent, the new concrete structures have created a fluid, multi-use space that has a 'quiet brutalism'.

Above Concrete plinths form benches and desks and the greenery provides both transparent partitions and a lush outlook for staff. **Opposite** The plants, very deliberately growing from the building itself, create 'places to pause, to learn and to converse', such as this padded seating nook.

House in the Outskirts of Brussels

BRUSSELS, BELGIUM
COMPLETED 2007

PHOTOGRAPHY
Marie-Françoise Plissart and Vincent Everarts

Above A glass facade at the rear of the property takes advantage of unobstructed views to nature and brings natural light into the interior. **Opposite** The second level houses six loft-like bedrooms, including the master and children's rooms. **Previous spread** The architects collaborated with a botanical artist to create the incredible green skin that encases the building and provides privacy from the neighbours.

This impressive home in the outlying suburbs of Brussels is largely encased in a living green skin. Creating privacy from nearby homes was important, and the architects state that, 'A completely vegetated volume facing the neighbours to the east of the building was an obvious choice.' This unusual cladding extends through to the north, east and south facades and along the roof. At the west-facing rear of the property, a dramatically different approach has been taken. 'The land to the west offers an unobstructed view of nature, which leads to the all-glass west facade.'

ARCHITECT
SAMYN and PARTNERS

BOTANICAL ARTIST
Patrick Blanc

Above The main bedroom features plywood cladding, timber flooring and a curved, slatted timber ceiling.
Opposite A carefully positioned array of exotic plants results in a beautifully textured effect, displaying movement and depth.

Internally, a thoughtful and generous layout includes an entry hall, family room, kitchen and living room spread across the original small building and the grand extension. On the second floor is the grand master bedroom with an ensuite, and five double-height children's rooms, each with a mezzanine and ensuite. Underground is a productive workspace, housing professional studios for the cinematographer owner.

According to the architects, 'Initially, the plan was simply to cover the building with Virginia creeper, as is traditionally found on older buildings in Belgium. However, the client introduced [us] to Patrick Blanc in Paris, and a friendly and fruitful collaboration was born.' Patrick Blanc – botanical artist, botanist and one of the most prominent proponents of vertical gardening – was developing a lighter-weight hydroponic green-wall system that was light enough to be used in a setting such as this. His new design has revolutionised green walls around the world. This system sees plants attached to a felt-like lining that covers the waterproofed facade. A network of small pipes supplies nutrient-rich water to the plants, which is then collected in a moat that runs along the foot of the vertical garden before being recycled back into the system.

Knowing that this would add additional weight – even though it was lighter than a traditional vertical or roof garden – the architects designed the home (apart from the external load-bearing walls) with lightweight wooden structures. This less-insulating material was offset by the thermal regulation provided by the green walls and roof.

Along with their more practical qualities, Patrick's green walls are living works of art. In this instance, he landed on a selection of species that are intricately positioned and layered to create a lush facade full of texture, depth and movement. Grass species like lesser pond sedge (*Carex acutiformis*) sit aside the herbaceous perennials bigroot geranium (*Geranium macrorrhizum*) and foamy bells (*Heucherella* 'Quicksilver'). The decorative foliage of variegated plantain lily (*Hosta* cv.) and tri-colour sage (*Salvia officinalis* 'Tricolor') add interest and complement shrubs such as myrtle-leaved willow (*Salix bockii*) and oakleaf hydrangea (*Hydrangea quercifolia*). Patrick's extensive plant knowledge ensures these species will thrive in this unusual setting. Together, the design team have created a building that is part botanical installation, part eco-system, part welcoming family home.

This lightweight hydroponic green-wall system has revolutionised the vertical garden and green wall industry. A variety of grass species, herbaceous perennials and decorative foliage plants were chosen for their beauty as well as their ability to thrive in these unusual conditions.

River House

HAWTHORN, VICTORIA, AUSTRALIA
COMPLETED 2022

Traditional Owners: Wurundjeri Woi-wurrung people of the Kulin Nation

PHOTOGRAPHY
Lisa Cohen

ARCHITECT
Susi Leeton Architects + Interiors

LANDSCAPE DESIGNER
Myles Baldwin Design

BUILDER
Skilcon

Occupying a steep and incredibly lush site that slopes down to a bend on Melbourne's iconic Yarra River, the design for this generous family home is a direct response to the landscape in which it sits. According to architect Susi Leeton, 'every aspect of the project was informed by the beautiful site'. As a neighbour-turned-friend of the home's owners and their then-young family, Susi was first engaged in a renovation of River House more than fifteen years ago. With their children now teenagers, Susi was the owners' first choice to reimagine the site to suit their evolved family dynamic. The goal was to create a space that fostered a stronger connection between each other as well as to the landscape.

Right The lush roof garden conceals the garage. **Below** The landscaping uses a minimal, green and white palette that complements the architecture, allowing both elements to shine. **Opposite** The pool cantilevers out from a top-floor terrace. **Previous spread** Sculptures by Isadora Vaughan sit beside a Japanese maple in the hallway.

Below The living space has a decidedly green outlook and features impressive artworks by Australian artists Daniel Boyd (back wall) and Kevin Chin (beside fireplace) alongside Italian design classics such as the B&B Italia Camaleonda Sofa. **Opposite** Large frameless glazing throughout the house celebrates the verdant view and blurs the boundary between inside and out.

Left (top) Beautiful specimen trees provide a forest-like setting. **Left (bottom)** A smoky mirrored cube conceals the pantry and bar, and reflects the landscape into the room. **Opposite** The glazed roof over the kitchen and breakfast nook brings the outside in, taking advantage of the views of trees and sky. **Following spread** Every level and room looks to the garden and the surrounding parkland, providing seclusion and an ever-present connection to nature.

Gently meandering down to the river over five levels, the house – despite its size – recedes beautifully into its surroundings, embedding itself in the greenery. The first glimpse of the home from the path is of the densely planted roof garden that conceals the garage, where plants tumble gently over the building's edge. It is clear from the outset that greenery inside and out plays a pivotal role in this home.

The brief to landscape designer Myles Baldwin and his team was, as Myles explains, to 'draw the adjacent parkland surrounding into the property with an emphasis on beautiful specimen trees providing a forest-like setting'. This approach provides privacy from neighbouring apartments and maximises the green outlook from the house.

At every juncture of River House there is a deference to nature, from the ever-present connection to the verdant garden with its 'considered understorey plantings, tree canopies, rooftop planters and placement of pots' to the inclusion of a Japanese maple (*Acer palmatum*) that grows out of the indoor oak flooring. The maple's deciduous leaves are a constant reminder of seasonality and natural beauty.

A deliberately muted palette of robust yet minimal materials provides the perfect background to family life. It grounds the spaces and avoids distraction from the surrounding landscape. Similarly, the colour scheme of the landscaping is kept minimal with an array of greens and white. Plants such as kidney weed (*Dichondra repens*), creeping fig (*Ficus pumila*), oakleaf hydrangea (*Hydrangea quercifolia*) and oyster plant (*Acanthus mollis*) complement the architecture, allowing both elements to shine. Large frameless windows that create paintings of the ever-changing views beyond maximise natural light in the space and help to beautifully blur the external edges of the building. Smoky mirrors and polished plaster walls reflect natural light and views of greenery.

At every juncture of River House there is a deference to nature.

Often undervalued, southern light is embraced at River House – it shifts and moves during the day and through the seasons. This is combined with skylights that are used to great effect to bring natural light deep into the interior spaces, reducing the need for artificial lighting during the day. One such opening provides beautifully diffused light to the Japanese maple below, and the glass roof in the kitchen offers clear views to trees and sky above. By prioritising views to the environment over the architecture, a real sense of immersion within the landscape has been created, emphasising the feeling of seclusion despite the house's close proximity to the city.

River House celebrates a holistic approach to design, one that examines the project as a whole 'conscious of how a space (and) a landscape makes you feel'. The process is cognisant of all five senses, responding to light, sounds, sunshine, a view to greenery and sky, the wind and the seasons. In many ways the architecture becomes a backdrop to the landscape and the result, in Susi's words, is a 'space that makes you exhale when you walk in the door'.

VIVIENNE
Wisdom Andrew Zuckerman

Above The lift that opens to an outside walkway surrounded by greenery aids accessibility to this five-level home. **Opposite** Despite its grand size, River House blends beautifully into its lush surrounds thanks to a design that prioritises a connection between nature and the built form. **Previous spread** The master bedroom enjoys sweeping views to the canopy of the surrounding trees through floor-to-ceiling glazing.

Featherston House

IVANHOE, VICTORIA, AUSTRALIA
COMPLETED 1969 (ORIGINAL); 2019 (ALTERATION)

Traditional Owners: Wurundjeri Woi-wurrung people of the Kulin Nation

PHOTOGRAPHY
John Gollings

Above and opposite At Featherston House – surrounded by bush and with an abundant garden growing inside – nature is an ever-present ideally not alone **Previous spread** The flourishing passionfruit vine in the indoor garden uses steel cables to climb to the roof.

Undoubtedly one of Melbourne's most significant homes, Featherston House was designed by architectural icon Robin Boyd for the equally iconic designers Grant and Mary Featherston. Full of creativity and playfulness, the home was originally commissioned by Grant and Mary in 1967 as a space for living, working and entertaining. It is now occupied by their son Julian, his wife, Vicky, and their young family.

ARCHITECT
Robin Boyd (original); Featherston family (alteration)

INTERIOR ARCHITECT/ DESIGNER
Mary and Grant Featherston (original); Featherston family (alteration)

LANDSCAPE DESIGNER
Featherston family

Right (top) The relocated master bedroom sits beneath the living platform and is surrounded by lush greenery. **Right (bottom)** View of the children's play area and bedroom from the main part of the house. **Opposite** View from the pond and internal garden to the glazed facade and an expansive bush outlook.

Robin Boyd was a pioneer of modernist design in Australia. An architect, educator and writer, he was prolific in his output and advocated for a distinctly Australian style of design. Mary and Grant, famous for their furniture, interior and graphic design, were open-minded when it came to the brief for their new home, hoping only that it would foster a connection between family, work and nature.

Encased in a deceptively simple shell of brick and translucent polycarbonate sheeting, the internal structure is set over various meandering levels, each platform serving a distinct purpose and virtually hovering over the one below while remaining open to the building at large. To the south, a multi-level, floor-to-ceiling, wall-to-wall window has views of the native garden and bushy landscape beyond. As well as outlook, the wall of glass allows an abundance of light to filter through to the living spaces and the internal garden below.

Rising from ground level alongside a large pond and creeping up beside a staircase, the extensive internal garden is one of the most strikingly modern features of this home. Unusually, as the building is not sitting on a slab of concrete, the soil that makes up its base is directly connected to the earth below. Heavily patterned peacock plant (*Goeppertia makoyana*) and never never plant (*Ctenanthe* spp.) mingle with flowering bird of paradise (*Strelitzia reginae*), climbing Swiss cheese vine (*Monstera adansonii*), round-leafed Chinese money plant (*Pilea peperomioides*) and radiator plant (*Peperomia* spp.). Ferns like maidenhair (*Adiantum aethiopicum*), silver lady (*Blechnum gibbum*) and bird's nest (*Asplenium nidus*) sprawl among a dense bed of spike moss (*Selaginella* spp.) and baby's tears (*Soleirolia soleirolii*), while passion flowers (*Passiflora* spp.) climb up wire supports towards the ceiling.

Nature is everywhere, from the indoor garden to the views of bush and sky, the sounds of the local wildlife and the light pouring through the translucent roof. Natural materials have also been employed. Vicky says that the idea of 'truth to materials' was part of the original concept, which they have tried to retain over the lifespan of the house. There are very few painted surfaces and colours are broadly kept to their natural material colour.

Julian and Vicky recently completed a renovation that respects the original design of Featherston House while modernising it to suit their family's lifestyle. The reworking has also allowed them to more successfully realise some of Boyd's original vision through the use of updated technology. Mary now lives in an apartment attached to the original home. Designed by Julian, this replaces an older apartment previously inhabited by her own parents. This is a true design classic, and it is admirable to see it passed with such reverence from one generation to the next.

The interior spaces of Featherston House are designed as a series of open platforms that all have a distinct purpose. With each platform hovering over the one below, the space remains beautifully open and expansive. In this house's most recent iteration, the lower ground area was excavated to make room for the master bedroom. As a result, the indoor garden had to be completely replanted.

Edgeland House

AUSTIN, TEXAS, USA
COMPLETED 2012

PHOTOGRAPHY
Paul Bardagjy

ARCHITECT
Bercy Chen Studio
LANDSCAPE CONSULTANT
Lady Bird Johnson Wildflower Center
BUILDER
Bercy Chen Studio

Edgeland House, located in Austin, Texas, is a masterclass in regenerative architecture. What was once an industrial site littered with debris with a disused, asbestos-covered oil pipeline running through its centre, is now a well-loved home replete with a thriving ecosystem filled with indigenous plants and wildlife. Thomas Bercy and Calvin Chen of Bercy Chen Studio say the design of this home was based on the idea of 'healing the land and ameliorating the scars of the site's industrial past'.

Right View through the dining area to the main entrance. **Below** The lines of the pool draw the eye to the surrounding landscape. **Opposite** A once debris-littered site now sustains a thriving ecosystem of native flora and fauna. **Previous spread** Loosely inspired by the Native American pit house, the house is built into the ground to mitigate uncomfortable temperature extremes.

Right (top) View to the pool through the slim courtyard.
Right (bottom) The house is made up of two separate pavilions for living and sleeping quarters – passing between them requires direct contact with the outside elements.
Opposite The triangular pool narrows to a point as it extends away from the house.

The site, which would have deterred many in its less-than-ideal state, was purchased by writer, lawyer and avid nature lover Christopher Brown to build a house on for himself and his son. Through the process of creating the home he met his wife, the architect and artist Agustina Rodriguez. The couple now have a young child. With Christopher having recently written the book *A Natural History of Empty Lots*, the family's interest in the wild spaces of so-called 'edgelands' is clear. With their architects, they have revitalised this lot and provided a fantastic model for others to do the same.

The design of Edgeland House is loosely inspired by the Native American pit house. Built into the ground, this style of structure, also found in various other cultures around the world, insulates the building from extreme temperatures. In response to the large excavation caused by the oil pipeline, the building was designed to sit within this break in the land, with a garden-covered rooftop restoring the original sloping of the landscape. The two halves of this home, with a slim courtyard between them, house living areas on one side and bedrooms and bathrooms on the other. To move from one side to the other, the occupants must pass through the outdoor space that separates them, ensuring a daily sense of connection to the environment.

For the planting of the rooftop garden, the architects collaborated with the Lady Bird Johnson Wildflower Center. This organisation, part of the University of Texas, is on a mission to 'inspire the conservation of native plants', using them to restore and create sustainable, beautiful landscapes for both public and private land. The aim is to 'improve water quality, provide habitat for wildlife, and enhance human health and happiness'.

The native gardens covering the site allow the architecture to read as an extension of the landscape and soften the striking angles and robust materials of the structure.

This area is part of the Texas Blackland Prairies, a temperate grassland that is one of the most endangered in North America. Indigenous to this habitat are grasses like splitbeard bluestem (*Andropogon ternarius*) and switchgrass (*Panicum virgatum*), and flowering plants such as meadow garlic (*Allium canadense* var. *mobilense*), old man's beard (*Clematis drummondii*), propeller flower (*Alophia drummondii*) and woolly Dutchman's pipe (*Aristolochia tomentosa*), exemplifying the great diversity of species in the region.

At Edgeland House, invasive species have been removed, soil has been restored, and more than forty local wildflower and grass species have been reintroduced to the site. According to the architects, these native species 'connect the home with the site and the seasons'. The building acts as an extension of the natural landscape, and the softness of these plants provide a perfect visual balance to the extensive use of glazing and concrete and the strikingly angular roof.

A testament to the thoughtful work of the owners and architects is the abundance of wildlife now finding a home on the site, from armadillos to butterflies. Nature is at the forefront of this design, allowing the site to reclaim what was once taken from it.

Fitzroy Community School Creative Space

THORNBURY, VICTORIA, AUSTRALIA
COMPLETED 2012

Traditional Owners: Wurundjeri Woi-wurrung people of the Kulin Nation

PHOTOGRAPHY
Rory Gardiner

Above The restrained material palette is elevated by greenery. **Opposite** The 'verandah', enclosed to the south and east in clear polycarbonate cladding, creates an all-weather space that remains connected to the surrounding greenery. Fragrant star jasmine grows up the timber structure within, creating a living green wall inside. **Previous spread** Plywood clads the interior core that houses the kitchen and library space, along with learning and teaching areas, offices and workshops.

It is vitally important to design educational buildings in a way that encourages and facilitates positive learning experiences. The success of these buildings lies in their ability to support the teaching approach of the organisations they house. The Fitzroy Community School Creative Space is the second campus of an independently owned, uniquely run primary school. It is used by a small group – around thirty-five children and their teachers. With an integral link to landscape and greenery, coupled with a focus on informal, interconnected multi-use spaces, it allows for a broad spectrum of activities in an environment that is more like a large family home than a school.

ARCHITECTS
Baracco+Wright Architects and Richard Stampton Architects

LANDSCAPE DESIGNERS
Baracco+Wright Architects and Richard Stampton Architects

BUILDER
Jeff Williams Building Services

Left (top) Gnomes enjoy one of the outdoor areas. This playful space encourages students to explore and learn in close proximity to nature. **Left (bottom)** Thanks to a design that leans towards the domestic, including a roof pitch that mimics those of the surrounding homes, the school fits seamlessly into its suburban locale. **Opposite** Landscaping was pivotal to the project, and it evolved alongside the design of the built form.

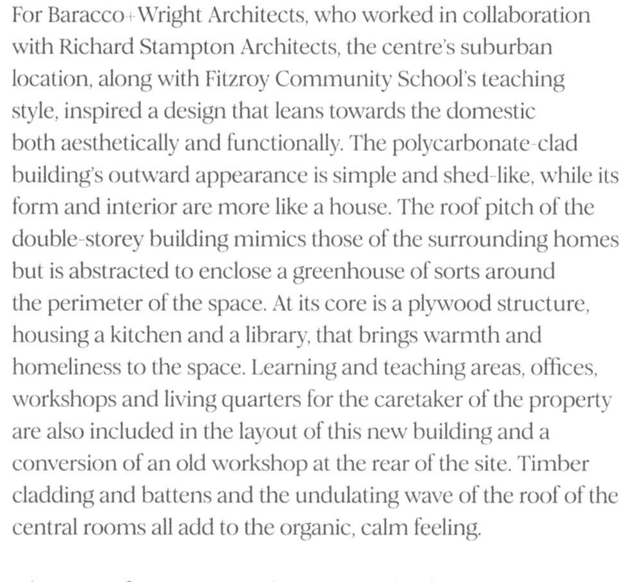

For Baracco+Wright Architects, who worked in collaboration with Richard Stampton Architects, the centre's suburban location, along with Fitzroy Community School's teaching style, inspired a design that leans towards the domestic both aesthetically and functionally. The polycarbonate-clad building's outward appearance is simple and shed-like, while its form and interior are more like a house. The roof pitch of the double-storey building mimics those of the surrounding homes but is abstracted to enclose a greenhouse of sorts around the perimeter of the space. At its core is a plywood structure, housing a kitchen and a library, that brings warmth and homeliness to the space. Learning and teaching areas, offices, workshops and living quarters for the caretaker of the property are also included in the layout of this new building and a conversion of an old workshop at the rear of the site. Timber cladding and battens and the undulating wave of the roof of the central rooms all add to the organic, calm feeling.

Like most of Baracco+Wright's projects, landscaping was an integral element in the design of this school and was planned alongside the architecture. The approach was not dissimilar to that of the architects' own holiday home (see Garden House on p. 124), with its polycarbonate shell that encases a perimeter 'verandah' – used to circulate around the building and connect to the surrounding greenery. Co-director of Baracco+Wright Architects, Louise Wright, explains, 'We find the informal spatial quality [of verandahs] suitable to Australian conditions and ways of using space, and of course, it brings one to the edge of the building in a more deconstructed and open way – closer to the landscape'.

Twelve years after completion, the Fitzroy Community School Creative Space has become well and truly ensconced in its site, softened beautifully by the now mature landscaping. Foliage from the trees facing the street, such as a snow gum (*Eucalyptus pauciflora*), gracefully dances across the facade, while star jasmine (*Trachelospermum jasminoides*) creeps upwards on the pillars between the cladding and the functional space of the verandah, creating a wall of deep green leaves and sweet-smelling flowers. Referencing the large backyards of the surrounding residential properties, the generous garden sits between the new street-facing building and the converted workshop at the rear of the site. There is a playfulness to this design, yet it is filled with a sense of calmness and quiet that is further enhanced by the thoughtful inclusion of plants. The building provides the perfect backdrop for children to explore the world around them, learning through everyday activities in an environment filled with creativity.

Above The simple shed-like form of the school is bold, yet in combination with the landscaping, which has matured beautifully, it feels delightfully unassuming and is very much ensconced in its site. **Following spread** At the rear of the building, a generous garden that references the surrounding suburban backyards offers more opportunities for play and connection with nature.

Landscaping was an integral element in the design of this school and was planned alongside the architecture.

Garden & House

TOKYO, JAPAN
COMPLETED 2011

PHOTOGRAPHY
Iwan Baan

ARCHITECT
Office of Ryue Nishizawa

Few cities are as densely populated as Tokyo, making its commercial district an unlikely site for a lush, light-filled townhouse. With a footprint of just 4 × 8 metres (13 × 26 feet) and surrounded on three sides by tall buildings, out-of-the-box thinking was required to create a combined home and workplace that maximised space, natural light and privacy for the owners.

Right The clever layout permits easy access to lush outdoor areas from all rooms and levels. **Below** The circular cutout in the rooftop garden allows light to enter below and provides extra growing room for mature plants. **Opposite** The striking white steel staircase cuts through the centre of the building and provides access to the concrete platform floors that make up this five-storey home. **Previous spread** Sandwiched between residential towers in Tokyo's commercial district, the house provides important green respite to the urban streetscape.

Right (top) The house reads as a vertical garden thanks to plant-filled terraces on every level. **Right (bottom)** View through the central staircase to a bedroom below. **Opposite** Sheer curtains create translucent partitions and enhance the sense of transparency throughout the home. **Following spread** The first-floor terrace features plants growing from inbuilt concrete planters alongside potted specimens, making it a productive workspace.

Ryue Nishizawa, director of the architecture firm Office of Ryue Nishizawa, has an extensive CV that includes a diverse range of residential, museum and hotel projects. With architect Kazuyo Sejima (co-founder of their combined studio SANAA), he has designed the Sydney Modern Project (the much-feted new wing of the Art Gallery of NSW) and the Musée du Louvre's sister gallery, Louvre Lens.

For this project, Office of Ryue Nishizawa arrived at a design solution that optimised the tiny site by using reinforced concrete platforms seemingly suspended on top of one another, thanks to discreet steel supports and three reinforced concrete columns. Set over five storeys, including an accessible rooftop, the house rises vertically via a staircase that cuts through the centre of the building. Bedrooms, living areas and workspaces are laid out to give the occupants easy access to the outside from both the private and public realms, allowing them to access fresh air and sunlight as they go about their daily activities.

Looking more like a vertical garden than a home, thanks to generous, plant-filled balconies and terraces facing the street, as well as internal planting, Garden & House brings life and verdancy to its decidedly urban locale. Tropical foliage, including umbrella plant (*Schefflera* spp.), banana plant (*Musa* spp.) and Swiss cheese plant (*Monstera deliciosa*), provides the perfect antidote to the harsh concrete and brick structures that dominate the streetscape.

Glazed facades that sit back from plant-filled terraces on each level protect the interior from the elements while allowing light to penetrate. Curtains, both internally and externally, provide privacy and partitions without sacrificing spaciousness. The softness of the material juxtaposes the solid concrete platforms maintaining the feeling of transparency that the house embodies.

Referencing qualities revered in traditional Japanese houses – a connection to natural elements, the absence of walls, and flexible planning – Garden & House elevates the lives of its occupants in an incredibly modern way. It is a green oasis wedged between offices and apartments that gives as much to the city as it does to its owners.

Corner House

FLINDERS, VICTORIA, AUSTRALIA
COMPLETED 2020

Traditional Owners: Bunurong/Boon Wurrung people of the Kulin Nation

PHOTOGRAPHY
Rory Gardiner

ARCHITECT
Archier

LANDSCAPE ARCHITECT
Openwork

BUILDER
PMV Built

Situated in the coastal town of Flinders, approximately 90 kilometres from Melbourne, Corner House inverts the traditional suburban house plan. Tasked with creating a new home for a retiring couple, architects Archier created a warm and inviting house that belies its relatively modest proportions. To mark this crucial change of lifestyle for the clients, who were relocating and leaving behind demanding architectural careers, Archier wanted to not only accommodate but elevate the clients' evolving daily lives.

Right Living spaces are positioned in each corner of the aptly named Corner House. **Below** The compact and cosy lounge room looks out to the foliage of mature trees. **Opposite** The central courtyard operates as another 'room' within the house, with the landscaping providing a subtle sense of privacy between the interior spaces. **Previous spread** View to the office from the courtyard. **Following spread** Gradual changes in levels allow for a private guest space, ensuite and storage beneath the living space.

Above (left) The bathroom overlooks the courtyard, promising a tranquil bathing experience. **Above (right)** The high ceiling and full-length glazing in the study makes it feel spacious. **Opposite** The double-height master bedroom looks out to a mature Chinese tallow tree.

Despite its proximity to the stunning coastline of the Mornington Peninsula, the site is on a main road and views are obscured by large residential developments that flank it on both sides. This led the architects to design a home that looks inward rather than out and centres around an impressive courtyard. This protected outdoor space extends views to the internal garden across the site, successfully bringing the outside in and ensuring privacy from neighbours.

Corner House derives its name from its layout. The uniquely shaped site allowed the architects to work with a square footprint, placing each of the main rooms – studio, bedroom, kitchen/dining, and lounge – in one of its four corners. Extensive glazing in these rooms contrasts with the long, enclosed corridors that extend along the perimeter of the building. These passageways, which connect the rooms without the need for doors, provide ample wall space for the couple's art collection and add to the dynamic experience of moving through the house. This interplay of hiding and exposing spaces also enhances the impact when the view to the landscape is revealed.

The facade of the home references the board-and-batten detail of typical Flinders fishing cottages, while the internal and courtyard areas make liberal use of timber and glass. Blackbutt flooring and joinery, and sustainably sourced Victorian ash windows and doors, create a harmonious, natural feel. The glass – double glazed for maximum thermal efficiency – allows the inhabitants to observe each other from the separate spaces and also gaze at the calming courtyard garden.

The courtyard planting has a distinctively Japanese feel and the chosen species change colour with the passing seasons, meaning a constantly evolving view. The lush landscaping is the handiwork of the Melbourne-based landscape architectural consultancy Openwork. Anchoring the space are three mature trees – a Chinese tallow (*Triadica sebifera*), a dogwood (*Cornus* sp.), and an Adriatic fig (*Ficus carica* 'White Adriatic') – all of significance to the owners. The large canopies of foliage sit beautifully against the timber cladding and glazing, softly obscuring views and giving a subtle sense of privacy between the interior spaces. Corner House is a masterclass in how to design a home and garden that are deeply connected to one another.

Below Sitting on a main road and flanked by large residential developments, Corner House looks inwards rather than out. From the exterior, it appears as a minimal cube concealing a lush centre. **Opposite** Circulation in the house is via passageways around the perimeter. The enclosed corridors contrast with the open living spaces and their walls display the owners' impressive art collection.

House of the Big Arch

WATERBERG, LIMPOPO, SOUTH AFRICA
COMPLETED 2019

PHOTOGRAPHY
Frankie Pappas and Dook Clunies-Ross

Above A simple selection of materials enables the building to fit seamlessly within its site. Rough stock brick that matches the site's weathered sandstone is used in abundance alongside sustainably sourced timber. **Opposite** Occupying a unique site in a nature reserve, the house disappears into this remarkable landscape. **Previous spread** The footprint of the building weaves around existing trees on the site – incredibly, not a single tree was destroyed in the construction of the house.

Architecture collective Frankie Pappas approached the design and build of House of the Big Arch with an important mission: to ensure minimal disruption to the landscape. Located in a mountainous nature reserve in Waterberg, South Africa, respecting and honouring the land was of utmost importance to architects and owners alike. This is a treehouse like no other – as architect and founding member of Frankie Pappas Ant Vervoort explains, it coexists alongside 'remarkable plants, inspiring cliffs, and prodigious wildlife'.

ARCHITECT
Frankie Pappas

Below A treehouse like no other, the building connects the landscape between forest and sandstone cliff, allowing the living spaces to sit high within the foliage surrounded by an abundance of wildlife. **Opposite** The timber bridging that spans the brick structures reduces both the footprint and impact of the building.

Right (top) The cellar under the arch has a climate that is ideal for curing meats, storing food supplies and ageing wines.
Right (bottom) A tree-shaded deck with a spectacular view features a fireplace where the majority of cooking is done.
Opposite View out and up from the dramatic entrance.

Sitting between a sandstone cliff and wild riverine forest, the location helped to define the brief: to design a home that disappeared into the surrounding bush and provided shelter not just for its human occupants but also for the abundant wildlife that calls this region home.

Relatively slim living and sleeping spaces are connected by walkways, many raised above the ground so as not to interrupt the movement of animals and insects along the bush floor. The long, thin shape of the building is a product of the team's desire not to fell any trees during the build. During the design stage they mapped out every tree and branch on the site and then organised a footprint that weaved around them. Incredibly, they were successful in their mission not to damage any of the existing trees, which include species such as paperbark false-thorn (*Albizia tanganyicensis*) and fever tree (*Vachellia xanthophloea*).

This is an off-grid home. Water is collected and recycled and energy is supplied via solar panels. Employing passive design principles led to smartly considered shade and ample ventilation that reduced energy needs. Material selection was also key. Ant explains, 'The building makes use of a very simple set of materials which all play their part in making the building part of its landscape. The most abundant material is a rough stock brick, which was selected to match the site's weathered sandstone.' Materials had to be hard-wearing and easy to deliver to the isolated site. Glass, aluminium and sustainably grown timbers add to the home's harmonious relationship with the surrounding landscape.

The owners – Ant's parents – are veterinarians and true nature lovers. Their passion for sharing their extensive knowledge of and enthusiasm for the local ecosystems sees them regularly opening their property to local underprivileged children. Their generosity to the site and their local community is testament to their kind nature. They simply say, 'There is too much beauty here for us to use up all by ourselves.'

Fisherman's House

BIRCHGROVE, NEW SOUTH WALES, AUSTRALIA
COMPLETED 2023

Traditional Owners: Wangal people of the Eora Nation

PHOTOGRAPHY
Gavin Green

Above The infinity pool merges seamlessly with the river beyond. **Opposite** The sandstone cliff face is revealed in a timber-clad nook in the new extension. **Previous spread** This three-storey concrete tower cleverly links the street to the original building at the water's edge. Indigenous plant species were sourced for the hanging gardens along the facade of the concrete tower – as they mature, they will reclaim the site.

ARCHITECT
Studio Prineas

LANDSCAPE DESIGNER
Bushy Landscapes

BUILDER
Dean Panos

This is a home of two halves, a home that is perfectly linked, a home of juxtapositions that fit together seamlessly and harmoniously on an unusual site. The owners, Dean Panos and Raquel Pittro, are long-time friends of Eva-Marie Prineas, principal of architecture firm Studio Prineas. The trio worked together on previous projects and were already in conversation about a new project when they came across an unusual site – a dilapidated fisherman's cottage, sitting below a sandstone cliff, about 9 metres (30 feet) from street level.

Left (top) The study features an Eames lounge chair and ottoman and looks out to a narrow green corridor. **Left (bottom)** The off-form concrete tower hugs the sandstone cliff. **Opposite** The planting not only regenerated the natural elements of the site, but plays an important role in bringing together the two separate entities that make up this home.

Although not officially protected by any heritage listing, the 19th-century cottage is a rarity on the Balmain peninsula. Out of respect for its history, the architects and owners decided that, instead of bulldozing the building, they would restore it. Space for the owners' family was achieved by adding a three-storey off-form concrete tower that clings to the cliff behind.

From the street, the home is incredibly discreet. A simple platform for parking and an intriguing little portal to a lift allow passers-by an uninterrupted view across the water to Cockatoo Island. On exiting the lift, you enter the new concrete structure, housing the bedrooms, study and wine cellar, all with views across the water or back to the sandstone. Hanging gardens sprout from the windowsills and vines cascade from them.

From the ground floor of the new extension, a glazed corridor carries you to the renewed open-plan cottage that sits on the waterfront. Full of heritage details, it houses the living, dining and kitchen spaces, embracing brilliant afternoon light and coastal views.

The guiding principles for the architects and landscape designers were regeneration and rehabilitation. Studio Prineas removed aluminium cladding and plaster from internal and external walls to reveal the original weatherboard, timber walls and floors, which were all sensitively restored. Sandstone blocks unearthed during the build have become the wall surrounding the waterfront pool.

Along with the original cottage, the owners also wanted to rehabilitate the natural landscape. Bushy Landscapes, a multidisciplinary team of bush regenerators, ecologists, landscapers, horticulturalists and designers was brought in. Liz Smith, ecologist and co-founder (alongside Erryn Blacklock) explains that 'the considered design set out to honour the historical context of the property both in its built and natural form, creating a home with a sophisticated, modern aesthetic that seamlessly integrates with its past'. An important part of Bushy's process is to undertake historical analyses and ecological surveys of the property and surrounding areas. This led them to design a reconstruction of Sydney's foreshore forests and coastal heaths on this waterfront Birchgrove site.

Below The original internal walls of the cottage were removed to create an open space for the kitchen, living and dining areas. In a nod to the building's origins, the exposed steel framework marks the location of the removed walls. **Opposite** Smoked oak timber veneer in the kitchen is sleek and sophisticated, providing moodiness in the otherwise light-filled space.

Above (left) Mirrored surfaces create an illusion of depth, while movable leather-clad doors provide flexibility in the modestly proportioned tower. **Above (right)** Custom timber joinery was used to build a compact workspace within a bedroom. **Opposite** The master bedroom enjoys spectacular river views, and a raised green marble bath that connects to the bedhead divides the room elegantly.

Bushy endeavours to regenerate remnant native vegetation wherever possible. Liz says, 'Heavily disturbed sites are completely reconstructed through the use of soil translocation, direct seeding and, of course, planting.' Along with concrete planter boxes across two floors of the extension, a courtyard garden on both sides of the glass corridor offers refuge from the heat of the afternoon sun and encourages a relationship between the two vastly different buildings.

Biodiversity is a key factor when creating ecologically sound gardens. Bushy has planted a rich range of endemic species – sixty-seven in total across this property, including pomax (*Pomax umbellata*), fuchsia heath (*Epacris longiflora*), narrow-leafed geebung (*Persoonia linearis*), wrinkled kerrawang (*Commersonia hermanniifolia*), threeawn speargrass (*Aristida vagans*), flannel flower (*Actinotus helianthi*), bat's wing fern (*Histiopteris incisa*), native fuchsia (*Correa reflexa*) and jungle grape (*Cissus hypoglauca*).

The new build could not be more different from the original cottage, yet it fits perfectly in place. The native and endemic species reintroduced throughout the site are slowly starting to flourish, restoring the former landscape and seamlessly melding the two buildings that make up Fisherman's House.

Above A glazed corridor links the new concrete building to the restored cottage at this thoughtfully executed junction.
Opposite A bedroom on the ground floor of the extension opens to a small courtyard area that looks out to the timber cladding of the fisherman's cottage.

Vivarium

THORNBURY, VICTORIA, AUSTRALIA
COMPLETED 2019

Traditional Owners: Wurundjeri Woi-wurrung people of the Kulin Nation

PHOTOGRAPHY
Tom Ross

ARCHITECT
Architecture architecture

LANDSCAPE ARCHITECT
Bush Projects

BUILDER
Bresnan & Smith

A serene and peaceful extension to an existing cottage in Melbourne's inner-north suburb of Thornbury, Vivarium is a perfectly formed home for a nature-loving family of four. 'Vivarium' is Latin for 'place of life' and this is a home that embraces life and nature in many forms. Looking for a design that prioritised a connection to the landscape, implemented passive design principles, maintained a similar footprint and used low-toxic materials, the owners chose design firm Architecture architecture because of their shared values around sustainability and biophilic design principles.

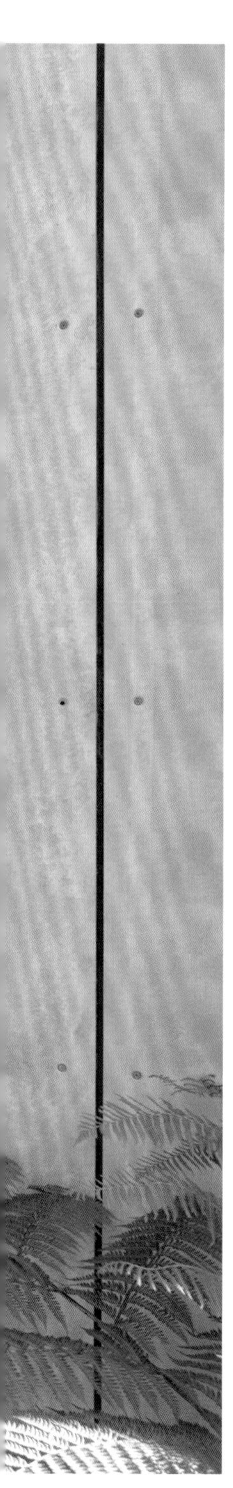

Right A tree grows from a cutout in the concrete floor of the dining space. **Below** The street frontage of the existing weatherboard cottage was largely maintained, concealing the modern addition to the rear. **Opposite** Looking into the kitchen and dining spaces from an exterior window seat, the extensive views to greenery are evident. **Previous spread** The design prioritises a connection to the landscape, encouraging the native garden to spill into the interior.

Left (top) The kitchen and other internal spaces feature durable low-toxic materials, including plywood, stainless steel and magnesium oxychloride. **Left (bottom)** As light shifts through the space throughout the day, flexible timber screening provides shade inside. **Opposite** The organic curves of the new addition work harmoniously with the textural landscaping. **Following spread** Extensive facades of curved glazing fill the new addition with natural light and invite the natural world in.

Opting to take minimal space for the additional building requirements, the architects reoriented the house to face the neighbouring park and reworked the floor plan to connect the house with the landscape at every juncture. Although modest in size, there is an undeniable spaciousness to the living areas thanks to smart planning. The space is both open yet defined by changes in floor levels and materials. Prioritising the nature of the site over the built form also meant the remaining space could be reserved for outdoor living. In turn, the natural environment is encouraged to spill into leisure and living areas. Architect Michael Roper explains that this is a 'house that addresses its context, integrating with its setting and drawing the parkland into the private realms of the house and garden'.

Working harmoniously with batches of native garden, the form of the new addition is sculptural and organic, thanks to gently curved timber and glass walls that invite the outside in. A lush central courtyard filled with textural planting brings light and life into the heart of the home. The landscaping is just as important as the built elements, and is the handiwork of multidisciplinary landscape architecture studio Bush Projects. Embraced by swathes of native grasses, including switchgrass (*Panicum virgatum* 'Heavy Metal'), the garden also includes gymea lily (*Doryanthes excelsa*) and groundcovers such as kidney weed (*Dichondra repens*) and creeping boobialla (*Myoporum parvifolium*), along with lots of indigenous wildflowers.

Minimal changes were made to the existing weatherboard cottage, respectfully maintaining its original street frontage and concealing the house's modern transformation. The main entrance was shifted to the side lane, at the intersection of the original house and the new extension. It is here that the reimagining of this home flourishes. A glazed hallway links the existing cottage with the new addition. This 'green corridor' from which all living and private spaces extend allows natural light to flood the space and offers an unobstructed view of the garden on entry. The new living areas, raised to address local flood levels, create a visual contrast between the old and new and have views of the neighbouring greenery. 'We decided to amplify this distinction and play to the parkland context by giving the extension a robust civic aesthetic, as well as expressing the height difference by allowing the garden to grow in under the house.'

Swathes of native grasses and a plethora of indigenous wildflowers are drawn into the internal living spaces by the sculptural timber screening.

Robust materials such as galvanised metal and cement sheet, and cyclone wire fencing, provide an urban palette that is softened by the site's natural elements. 'The galvanised sheet shimmers and reflects the colours of the parkland, while the black cyclone wire falls into shadow, permitting views between the garden and the park.' Inside, plywood, stainless steel and magnesium oxychloride wall linings were chosen for their durability as well as their low toxicity. Where possible, materials were locally sourced or repurposed to minimise waste.

Adopting passive design strategies, including integrated solar and ventilation systems, a large rainwater collection tank and the use of concrete flooring for thermal mass, helps limit the home's environmental impact by reducing running costs and maximising building performance. Movable timber screening adapts to light moving through the space during the day and increased shade will soon be provided by the vines growing along cables above the new addition. Michael believes that 'a project is only complete once it's enveloped in its landscape. Everything softens.'

Vivarium is a poetic response to the site and the owners brief, creating a dynamic, living building that has a positive impact on its occupants and the environment alike.

Barbican Conservatory

LONDON, ENGLAND, UK
COMPLETED 1982

PHOTOGRAPHY
Anna Batchelor

Above Small plants in terracotta pots sit on a vast windowsill. **Opposite** Spiderwort, spider plant and other trailing varieties cascade from a balcony and a Swiss cheese plant climbs up one of the many concrete pylons. **Previous spread** Home to over 2000 species of plants and trees, the Barbican Conservatory is a verdant oasis in the middle of London.

An icon of the brutalism movement, the Barbican Estate in central London is urban architecture at its best. Comprising apartments and townhouses for approximately 4000 residents, the complex also includes a performing arts centre, various eateries, a shallow artificial lake, a public library and, of course, the Barbican Conservatory. It is a visionary approach to modern living that is monumental in both size and concept.

ARCHITECT
Chamberlin, Powell and Bon

LANDSCAPE DESIGNER
Barbican Conservatory gardening team

BUILDER
John Laing Construction

The site was razed in the bombing of London during World War II, providing a blank canvas for architects Chamberlin, Powell and Bon (CPB). Initially employed as consultants on the project in the mid-1950s, CPB was officially appointed as the Barbican's architects in 1960. CPB's optimistic vision for the creation of a complex that encapsulated a modern neighbourhood reflected their ethos of architecture for the greater good. Numerous iterations of the Barbican's design were submitted and rejected until 1963, when construction of CPB's brutalist design finally began.

A philosophical, ethical and moral approach to building design, brutalism advocated honest, highly functional, less-decorative buildings. This style of building provided a sense of strength and stability and was a response to the devastation and uncertainty of war. The brutalist aesthetic is synonymous with large-scale, angular, monolithic forms, often hewn in concrete or other rough textures, and natural elements such as plants offset its severity.

CPB considered landscaping to be a vital component in the overall success of the Barbican, so it was a consideration from the outset of the design process. Species that would provide verdancy and interest throughout the seasons were specified and the gardens and water features throughout the complex bring much-needed softness and a reprieve from the harsh concrete that dominates the built structures. From inbuilt planters on the balconies of the residences to walkways lined with greenery, nature plays a starring role.

Designed in the brutalist aesthetic, the Barbican Estate uses lots of concrete and steel. Natural elements, such as plants and water features, offer a much-needed reprieve from the severity of the buildings.

Right (top) View through the conservatory's glass facade to one of the Barbican's residential towers. **Right (bottom)** Balconies within the conservatory have been consumed by greenery. **Opposite** Steps to a viewing platform.

This is most visible in the oasis that is the Conservatory – originally devised to cover the Barbican Theatre's fly tower (a structure that houses rigging and allows large sets to be delivered to the theatre below), in an effort to beautify the view from neighbouring buildings.

Sitting beneath 23,000 square feet (2137 square metres) of glass and steel roof, the Conservatory houses over 1500 species of plants, from the common Swiss cheese plant (*Monstera deliciosa*) and weeping fig (*Ficus benjamina*) to a collection of rare and endangered specimens. Arid House, which is attached to the main structure, is home to cacti and succulents, as well as a collection of *Cymbidium* orchids that hibernate during the cooler months. Some of these plants, including the giant Swiss cheese plant clambering up the side of the building, are over 40 years old.

The Conservatory, along with the green spaces within the broader Barbican Estate, provide a sense of calm and respite for its residents in an otherwise busy area of London. These spaces act as meeting places and form the social glue of this community. This vision of a modern inner-city neighbourhood, devised more than 60 years ago, still feels relevant today.

Resources

Architects + designers

07BEACH
@architecture_studio_07beach

act_romegialli
actromegialli.it

Amanda Oliver Gardens
amandaolivergardens.com.au

Anthony Gill Architects
gillarchitects.com.au

Archier
archier.com.au

Architecture architecture
architecturearchitecture.com.au

Baracco+Wright Architects
baraccowright.com

Bercy Chen Studio
bcarc.com

Bush Projects
bushprojects.com.au

Bushy Landscapes
bushylandscapes.com.au

Chamberlain Architecture & Interiors
chamberlainarchitects.com.au

Eckersley Garden Architecture
e-ga.com.au

FFLO
fflo.co.uk

Franchesca Watson
franchescawatson.com

Frankie Pappas
frankiepappas.com

Gheo Clavarino
gheoclavarino.it

Greenhouse Living
greenhouseliving.se

Hearth Studio
@hearthstudio

James Plumb
jamesplumb.co.uk

Lady Bird Johnson Wildflower Center
wildflower.org

LARC Landscape Architecture
larc.la

Michael Lumby Architecture
ml-a.co.za

Myles Baldwin Design
mylesbaldwin.com

Nielsen Jenkins
nielsenjenkins.com

Office of Ryue Nishizawa
ryuenishizawa.com

Openwork
openwork.info

Partners Hill
partnershill.com

Patrick Blanc
verticalgardenpatrickblanc.com

Pricegore
pricegore.co.uk

Retallack Thompson Architects
retallackthompson.com

Richard Stampton Architects
richardstampton.com

Robin Boyd
robinboyd.org.au

Robyn Barlow
robynbarlow.com

Ryan Klewer
@plantcharmer

Sacha Coles
aspect-studios.com

SAMYN and PARTNERS
samynandpartners.com

Setsquare Studio
setsquarestudio.com

Studio Bright
studiobright.com.au

Studio Prineas
studioprineas.com.au

Studio Rewild
@studiorewild

Susi Leeton Architects + Interiors
susileeton.com.au

Photographers

Anna Batchelor
annabatchelor.com

Bec Willox
@bec_willox

Ben Hosking
benhosking.com.au

Clinton Weaver
clinton-weaver.com

Dook Clunies-Ross
dookphoto.com

Frankie Pappas
frankiepappas.com

Gavin Green
gavingreen.com

Iwan Baan
iwan.com

Johan Dehlin
johandehlin.com

John Gollings
gollings.com.au

Karin Wildheim
wildheim.se

Lisa Cohen
lisacohenphotography.com

Marcello Mariana
marcellomariana.it

Martina Gemmola
gemmola.com

Marie-Françoise Plissart

Paul Bardagjy
bardagjyphoto.com

Phillip Huynh
@afloralfrenzy

Rory Gardiner
rory-gardiner.com

Tom Ross
tomross.xyz

Vincent Everarts
@vincent.everarts

Yosuke Ohtake
yosukeohtake.com

Builders & landscapers

Allstruct
allstructservices.com.au

Atma Builders
atmabuilders.com.au

Bresnan & Smith
bresnansmith.com.au

Castle Constructions
castleconstructionltd.com.au

Grenville Architectural Constructions
gaconstruct.com.au

Jeff Williams Building Services
jwbs.net.au

LARC Landscape Architecture
larc.la/

Melbourne Garages
melbournegarages.com.au

MIC Projects
micprojects.com.au

Munro Builds
munrobuilds.com.au

Nick Andrew Construction
@nickandrewconstruction

PMVBuilt
pmvbuilt.com.au

ProvanBuilt
provanbuilt.com.au

Roja Brimalm & Johan Holmstedt (owner-builders)
@husetivaxthuset

Skilcon
skilcon.com.au

Taylor and Ward
taylorandward.com.au

Further reading

Evergreen Architecture: Overgrown Buildings and Greener Living by gestalten (eds)
Field Notes (online at fieldnotes.christopherbrown.com) by Christopher Brown
Nature Inside: Plants and Flowers in the Modern Interior by Penny Sparke
The House of Green: Natural Homes and Biophilic Architecture by gestalten (eds)
The Planthunter: Truth, Beauty, Chaos and Plants by Georgina Reid
The Well Gardened Mind: Rediscovering Nature in the Modern World by Sue Stuart-Smith
Wonderground (online at wonderground.press) by Georgina Reid

Visual Index

16 DAYLESFORD LONGHOUSE

28 CHELSEA BRUT

38 GREEN BOX

AUTUMN HOUSE 46

58 HOUSE FOR A GARDEN

HOUSE IN KYOTO 78

MERRICK'S FARMHOUSE 66

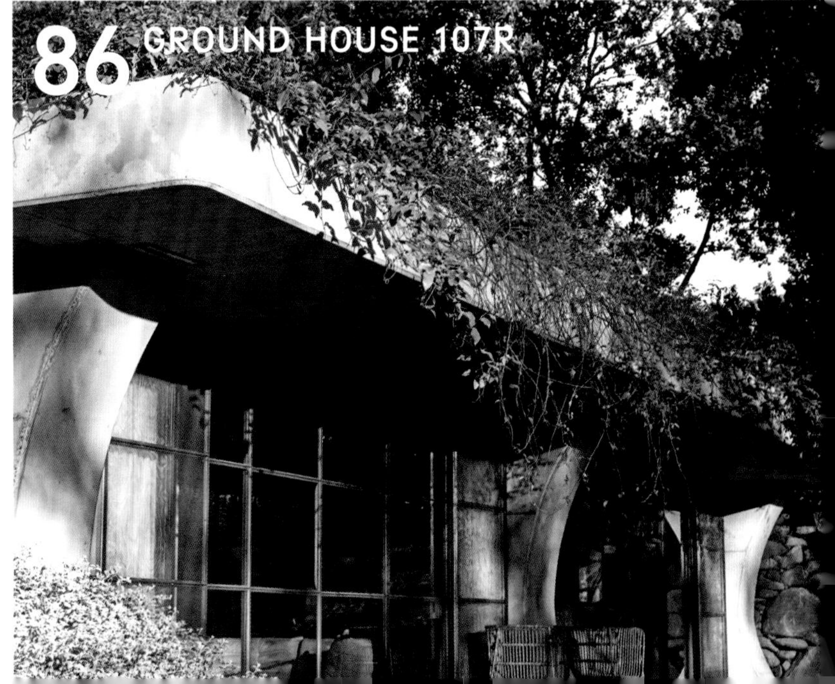
86 GROUND HOUSE 107R

PSLAB LONDON 144

162 RIVER HOUSE

154 HOUSE IN THE OUTSKIRTS OF BRUSSELS

FEATHERSTON HOUSE 176

HOUSE OF THE BIG ARCH 220

FISHERMAN'S HOUSE 228

240 VIVARIUM

250 BARBICAN CONSERVATORY

With thanks

We must start with our publisher, Paul McNally, a man sometimes brief in words, but full of faith in us. Thank you for continuing to trust us to create these books. Lorna Hendry, our editor, we are so grateful for the opportunity to work together again. We greatly appreciate your patience and skill in shaping our words. Thank you to project manager Elena Callcott for your help wrangling photography – no mean feat on a book like this.

To Georgina Reid, who so graciously wrote our foreword, we have long admired the way you see the world and the words and work you put out into it. We're honoured that your poetic prose begins our book.

Our huge and heartfelt thanks to all the architects, landscape designers, interior designers, builders and owners of these incredible buildings and landscapes for agreeing to have their work included in this book. It is a true honour to write about and publish these projects. Your generosity in helping to source details and photography for each project was immense. For those who took the time to answer our questions, we appreciate the thought that went into your responses. To the photographers who took the beautiful images that so perfectly capture the essence of each of these projects, thank you. Special mention to Rory Gardiner, Tom Ross and Clinton Weaver, whose work features across multiple projects.

SOPHIA I so enjoy creating these books – they have been an unexpected and immensely pleasurable part of my life and career. Thank you to Lauren for being a great co-creator and for all the careful consideration you put into the design of these pages. Thank you to my family for giving me the freedom to try all the things, to explore and learn and for supporting and encouraging me with every new project. Mum, Dad, Rosie, Olivia, Daniel, Trina, Leo, Alexia, Michael, Rafael and Otis, love you lots.

LAUREN Our books have a funny way of coinciding with pregnancies and births and this one was no exception. It would be impossible to find the time to work on these projects that mean so much, without the incredible support from my husband, Anthony, and parents, Maree and Richard. Baby Jack (and, of course, his big sister, Frankie) has been a beautiful distraction to time spent writing and designing our fifth book. And, of course, to Sophia – creating our books is a much more enjoyable experience with a partner in crime, especially throughout the writing process! Thank you for your epic production skills in pulling together our edit of projects and for taking the reins in the initial stages while I savoured the newborn bubble.

About the authors

Since 2018 Sophia and Lauren have published five books – *Leaf Supply*, *Indoor Jungle*, *Plantopedia*, *Bloom*, and now *Outside In*. Available worldwide, these books showcase their passion for plants and design.

Sophia is a floral stylist for editorial, commercial projects and events. She is currently studying horticulture and holds a Bachelor of Communications. Sophia loves learning about, exploring and getting her hands dirty in the weird, wonderful and enduringly romantic natural world around her.

Lauren is the creative director of *Belle* magazine and is the designer behind all of the pair's books. She holds a Bachelor of Interior Architecture and has had the privilege of working on a number of interior magazine titles. Her passion for architecture, interiors and (of course!) plants is undeniable.

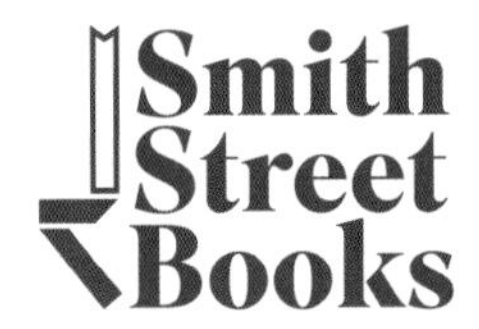

Published in 2024 by Smith Street Books

Naarm (Melbourne) | Australia

smithstreetbooks.com

ISBN: 978-1-9230-4955-0

Smith Street Books respectfully acknowledges the Wurundjeri People of the Kulin Nation, who are the Traditional Owners of the land on which we work, and we pay our respects to their Elders past and present.

Publisher: Paul McNally
Creative director: Lauren Camilleri
Cover designer: Murray Batten
Editor: Lorna Hendry
Proofreader: Pamela Dunne

Printed & bound in China by C&C Offset Printing Co., Ltd.

Book 349
10 9 8 7 6 5 4 3 2 1